Teaching Self-Control

A Curriculum for Responsible Behavior

Martin Henley, Ph.D.

Solution Tree

Cover design by Arc Group Ltd.

Text design and composition by T.G. Design Group

Printed in the United States of America

ISBN 1-932127-12-7

This book is dedicated to Nicholas Long—colleague, mentor, and friend.

ACKNOWLEDGMENTS

There is a widely held misconception that writers work alone. While it is true that much of the time a writer is physically alone, no manuscript is the work of only one person. Many educators provided feedback that enhanced this second edition of *Teaching Self-Control*. I owe special thanks to Brooke Wadhams, William Taynowski, and Maria Torres for helping to improve the sample lessons and report forms. My editor, Suzanne Kraszewski, never saw a citation she didn't care for. Her thoroughness and support was extraordinary. Most of all, I want to thank my wife, Teresa, for her patience, love, and extraordinary dinners. Many nights I emerged from my basement office tired, hungry, and strung-out. Teresa would put her arm around me, place a glass of wine in my hand, and say, "Dinner will be ready in about an hour, hon. Let's relax." That's how second editions get done.

CONTENTS

ABOUT THE AUTHOR

 Martin Henley, Ph.D., is a professor in the Education Department at Westfield State College and director of Pegasus Center for Education. He is a Vietnam veteran. After his war service, he was awarded two fellowships to Syracuse University where he earned an M.A. in special education with an emphasis in urban education and a Ph.D. in special education with an emphasis on students with emotional and behavioral disorders. His public school teaching career included positions in inner-city elementary schools and in special education; he was a Head Start director, and principal of Jowonio, an inclusive school for students with autism and serious emotional problems.

In addition to his teaching duties at Westfield State College, Dr. Henley has held various administrative positions including coordinator of special education undergraduate programs, director of graduate and continuing education special education programs, and chairman of the undergraduate college honors program. Dr. Henley is a frequent presenter at professional conferences and has published numerous articles on school discipline and violence prevention. He co-authored *Teaching Students With Mild Disabilities* with Roberta Ramsey and Robert Algozzine. Other books include *Creating Successful Inclusion Programs* and *Classroom Management: An Integrated Approach*.

Dr. Henley lives in Westfield, Massachusetts with his wife, Teresa, daughter, Maggie, and dog, Daisy. He is an avid runner and golfer.

FOREWORD

Children are not born with the skill of self-control. It is a skill that needs to be taught and learned. This is a complicated task because children are emotional, not rational, beings. During times of frustration, their emotions drive their behavior, causing a variety of problems for adults.

Historically, teaching self-control was not an issue for teachers, because the majority of students developed the foundations of self-control at home and the school needed only to reinforce them. But times have changed. Now thousands of students who have been neglected, rejected, and abused by their caregivers enter the classroom without the comfort and choice of being able to control their behavior during stressful times. Their negative attitudes and inappropriate behaviors, such as teasing their peers, not completing their assignments, and challenging authorities, guarantee they will have few teachers advocating their cause or promoting new programs for them.

What is alarming is the predictability of their pattern of self-defeating behavior. Without any educational intervention, these students will never experience the excitement of school achievement, the sense of autonomy, the joy of friendships, and the feeling of self-esteem. Without a caring and inclusive school staff who can see the misdeed of these impulsive students and teach them the skills of responsible behavior, there is little hope for them.

I congratulate Martin Henley for writing such a successful curriculum for teaching self-control in the classroom. This is not another armchair theory of self-control, but one that is based on actual studies with students. It is a strength-based functional approach—very realistic, reader friendly, easy to teach, and enjoyable for students. This curriculum not only promotes group cooperation and acceptance of others, but it is also the missing link for enhancing academic learning. As students learn to control their aggressive impulses and demonstrate new social skills, they will receive more peer and teacher approval, which in turn creates more energy and motivation to succeed at school. In plain language, the *Teaching Self-Control* curriculum provides a win-win situation for students and staff.

> —Nicholas Long, Ph.D.
> Professor Emeritus, American University
> President, The Life Space Crisis
> Intervention Institute

Self-Control

*There never has been, and cannot be, a good life
without self-control.*

— Leo Tolstoy

Each day, thousands of students come to school lacking the basic social skills needed for responsible behavior. They argue. They bully. They fight. They are unable to describe their feelings, check their anger, or control their impulses. Like rudderless boats tossed about on a rough sea, these children are unable to steer a course through their stormy emotions. Their inadequate academic skills add to their frustration and, in turn, to the turmoil they create in the classroom. Forty years ago, teachers harried students about gum chewing, running in the halls, and staying on the school grounds during recess. Today's teachers face students whose sense of the 3 R's is rage, resentment, and revenge.

No child is born violent. It takes many bad experiences to turn a youngster into a hostile student. For example, a developmental history of abuse or neglect is a strong predictor of violent behavior. Parents beating children, kids witnessing violence, and children selling their bodies for rent money sound like subplots in a horror story. Unfortunately, these are everyday events that fill the lives of many children, and the effects cause havoc in classrooms (see Figure 1.1). Consider the following scenes:

> *Eight-year-old Sylvia lives out of a paper sack. Each week she is shuttled from one relative to the next. When her teacher asks for homework, Sylvia yells, "F– – k you!" and runs out of the classroom. Sylvia is truant half the school year; and when she is in school, she is sleepy most of the time.*

> *Joshua is 9 years old. His cherubic face hardens like fast-drying cement when the principal confronts him with a stash of twenty-dollar bills recovered from his locker. "Whoa man, I work the streets hard for my money," he whines as he slumps in a chair, tears running down his cheeks.*

Daniel, age 15, believes his manhood rests on his ability to earn respect with his fists. "Like that f – – – ing boy disrespected me. So I punched him in the mouth. If he had kept his mouth shut, he would not of had my fist in it and he wouldn't have his teeth knocked out sucking on gauze right now." (Way, 1993, p. 5)

An entertainment industry that glorifies violence, grinding poverty that breeds crime, and inadequate parenting all contribute to irresponsible behavior. Just as there is no single cause, there is no single treatment. All segments of a youngster's life must be touched in order to quell the tidal wave of disruptive behavior that threatens public school classrooms.

For their part, schools can develop proactive classroom management systems that emphasize social skill development. This is not a new, add-on responsibility; schools have always required that students conform to specific rules of conduct. Teaching proactive social skills advances the traditional theme of fostering compliance to helping students develop their emotional intelligence.

EMOTIONAL INTELLIGENCE

Emotional intelligence refers to an individual's ability to monitor emotions and weigh alternatives before acting. Daniel Goleman (1995) explains the relationship between emotional intelligence and social skills:

> *Those who are at the mercy of impulse—who lack self-control— suffer a moral deficiency: The ability to control impulse is the base of will and character. By the same token, the root of altruism lies in empathy, the ability to read emotions in others; lacking a sense of another's need or despair, there is no caring. And if there are any two moral stances our times call for, they are precisely these, self-restraint and compassion. (p. xii)*

Emotionally intelligent individuals control their feelings, rather than letting their feelings control them.

Impulsiveness in childhood is a forerunner of aggression in adolescence and it undercuts social skill development. The Pittsburgh Youth Study tracked the delinquent careers of 1,517 boys for more than a decade. Researchers reported that impulsive judgment and impulsive behavior—more than any other individual trait such as IQ—were significantly and positively related to delinquency (Browning & Loeber, 1999). When Shoda, Mischel, and Peake (1990) tracked the developmental progress of impulsive 4-year-olds into adolescence, he found their lives filled with difficulties. They were easily frustrated. They were

Figure 1.1: AT-RISK FACTORS OF YOUTH IN THE UNITED STATES

- Over 900,000 children were confirmed victims of abuse and neglect in 1998.

- Black and Native American children are significantly over-represented among abuse and neglect victims—double their proportion in the national population.

- Three to ten million children witness family violence each year.

- Young children are most at risk for being abused and neglected. Infants represent the largest proportion of victims; almost 40% of victims are under age 6.

- A history of family violence or abuse is the single most significant contributor to delinquency.

- Children who witness domestic violence may display the following symptoms: sleep disorders, headaches, stomach aches, diarrhea, ulcers, asthma, enuresis, and depression. Such complaints are identified as reactions to stress.

- Children of women who are battered have high rates of poor school performance, truancy, absenteeism, and difficulty concentrating.

- Children who witness domestic violence experience symptoms such as anxiety, aggression, temperament problems, depression, low levels of empathy, and low self-esteem. Lower verbal, cognitive, and motor abilities are also documented as symptoms in children who witness domestic violence.

- Juveniles make up 71% of all sex crime victims reported to the police.

- In 1998, firearms killed 10 children every day. Of these, 2,184 were murdered, 1,241 committed suicide, and 262 were victims of accidental shootings.

- Between 1979 and 1998, gunfire killed nearly 84,000 children and teens in America—36,000 more than the total number of American soldiers killed in Vietnam.

- Not all children exposed to violence suffer significant harmful effects. Resilient factors include a protecting family member, a caring teacher, and supportive peers. Resilient factors also include a child's internal capacity to cope with stress.

Compiled from *America's Children: Key National Indicators of Well-Being,* by the Federal Interagency Forum on Child and Family Statistics (1999) and *A Month of Mental Health Facts: Fact-of-the-Day,* by the New York University Child Study Center (2001).

combative and unable to keep friends. A young person who is unable to control the impulse to strike out, either in fear or anger, is a walking powder keg. Almost half of the boys identified as bullies in elementary school will have adult felony records by age 24 (U.S. Department of Education, 1998).

Impulsive behavior is a survival mechanism that has been passed down to us from our ancient forebears. During the Paleolithic Era, an impulsive reaction could mean the difference between life and death. Making quick judgments and leaping to action was the best way to eat and avoid being eaten. The biological root of impulsiveness is located in the amygdala, a bundle of small almond-shaped glands near the base of the brain. The amygdala acts like a switching device. It instantaneously evaluates input from the senses and either forwards signals to the frontal lobe of the neocortex for further scrutiny or mobilizes the body for immediate response. The structure of this neural alert system is unchanged from the time our ancestors dressed in animal skins and slept in caves. Fate and the speed of cultural change have placed us in a fast-paced, complicated world with the brain of a cave dweller as our guide. Everyday life is filled with challenges to emotional intelligence. Frustrations, misunderstandings, and disappointments test our abilities to stay in control. Thinking before acting or speaking is the crux of emotional intelligence.

Emotional circuits may be configured by nature, but they are cultivated by experience. Practiced consideration helps to strengthen the neural pathways between the amygdala and the frontal lobe. For young people who are raised in households or neighborhoods where abrupt and hostile reactions are common, the neural track between the amygdala and the frontal lobe becomes the path least traveled. The amygdala kick-starts an impulsive youngster into action without regard for the consequences. Daniel Goleman (1995) calls this an "emotional hijacking." An atavistic reaction to a perceived threat elevates, rather than reduces, danger by turning impulse into aggression. An often-cited reason for aggressive behavior is a "knee-jerk" reaction to a perceived slight.

Acting out aggressive behavior characterizes three-quarters of students placed in special education programs because of a behavior or emotional problem (U.S. Department of Education, 1998). Impulsivity not only characterizes the behavior of many youth with mild disabilities, but it also influences how they think about themselves and the world around them. Rather than reflecting on how their impulsive behavior hurts others, aggressive youth rationalize their actions. These rationalizations distort their ability to put their behavior into a proper social perspective. They are unable to see their actions from any point of view other than their own. This "me-centeredness" plays a critical role in their low emotional intelligence. Students with behavior disorders in particular utilize self-serving thinking patterns to rationalize their behavior. These "cognitive distortions" serve as a sort of character armor, keeping at bay the slings and arrows of reality.

In the early 1990s, a female jogger was beaten and raped in Central Park. When interrogated by the police about their motive, the confessed attackers explained that they were "wilding" (i.e., having fun). Several of the youth pointed out that it was the jogger's fault she was attacked, because she should have known better than to be in the park during the evening. Such cognitive distortions twist reality into self-serving observations about victims (Henley & Long, 1999). Thus, a car is stolen because "he was stupid to leave the keys in the ignition"; a deliveryman is killed because a teen wants a new pair of shoes.

In her article "Do Conduct Disordered Gang Members Think Differently?" Beverly Lewis (1992) described the "errors in criminal thinking." Included among the rationalizations for their actions, aggressive youth blame their victims, and cite causes outside their control, such as poverty and insults (e.g., being "dissed"). Aggressive youth follow their own line of misguided logic, and their egocentric explanations are bereft of social conscience. Such children are delayed in their emotional intelligence. They maximize the fulfillment of immediate physical needs and desires, and they minimize their responsibility for their actions.

The absence of a comprehensive mental health system in this country, coupled with the staggering number of children (one in five) who grow up in poverty, presents a challenging picture for those who care about the social and emotional welfare of young people. In September 2000, Surgeon General David Satcher convened a national conference on children's mental health in Washington, D.C. Experts agreed that at best only one-half of young people with emotional problems receive professional help. Steven Hyman, Director of the Institute of Mental Health, implored educators to give students' mental health as much attention as their academic performance: "In education, cognitive development has been emphasized. In contrast, social and emotional development has been pushed under the rug . . ." (U.S. Public Health Service, 2000, p. 1). An appropriate educational response is needed to help at-risk students before they develop serious social and psychological problems.

TEACHING SELF-CONTROL

Although disruptive youngsters demonstrate a range of behavioral and emotional problems, it is their lack of self-control that causes the greatest difficulty in school—both for themselves and for their teachers (Goleman, 1995). Traditional discipline strategies do not work with students whose life histories have hardened them to threats and punishment. These students present a challenge to the most sanguine teacher. The meager doses of discomfort doled out by school discipline codes barely make a dent in these students' armor-plated personalities. Confront them and they fight back. Punish them and they grow resentful. Suspend them and they are back on the streets, where they continue to relearn all the wrong lessons for getting along in life.

What is a teacher to do when confronted with students who lack basic social skills for controlling their behavior and getting along with others?

The solution is simple and direct: *teachers can do what they do best—teach.* The same skills that teachers bring to mathematics, reading, and science can be incorporated into a social-skills curriculum that builds self-control. Self-control can be taught directly through lessons and activities, and it can be taught indirectly through routines, discussions, and a cooperative classroom climate.

Not long ago, I was speaking at a teacher conference when a teacher objected, "Teaching self-control sounds fine," she said, "but I have my hands full teaching math, reading, and everything else. Now you tell me I should be teaching social skills as well. That's the family's job, not mine." I welcomed this comment because I believe this teacher was speaking on behalf of many who feel overwhelmed. Such imperatives as "raise achievement scores," "establish inclusive classrooms," "respect multicultural issues," and "keep your classroom under control" seem overwhelming. The implication is that teachers should conjure a formula for solving society's problems. With the pressure of so many expectations, why should teachers accept the additional burden of teaching students self-control?

Teachers do not have to start teaching self-control—they already are doing it. Self-control is a hidden curriculum in every public-school classroom. Classroom management, which goes on every moment of every school day, is permeated with hundreds of mini-lessons about self-control.

The problem is that much of this incidental teaching is unfocused. Its potential is lost because of a lack of clarity about the specific social skills that constitute self-control.

WHAT IS SELF-CONTROL?

In many classrooms, the most visible indicator of a self-control curriculum is the list of class rules taped to the wall. The problem with this traditional practice of posting rules to guide behavior is apparent only when one examines teachers' expectations for how their students should act. As an illustration, let's examine two different scenarios:

> *In Ms. Whitney's classroom, rules remind students not to talk, to raise their hands if they want help, and not to get out of their seats without teacher permission. Compliance is the prized behavior. Students who break the rules get their names written on the blackboard, and a check is made after their names following each subsequent misdeed. If students accumulate more than three checks in a day, they have to serve detention at the end of the day for punishment.*

In Ms. Loop's classroom, the rules are developed jointly by the teacher and students. Students are reminded to help each other, to share ideas, and to take responsibility for classroom tasks. Cooperation is the desired behavior. Consequences are linked to the misconduct. A student who disrupts a classroom discussion must leave the group and work alone. A student who bullies another on the playground loses recess for two days. Ms. Loop looks for causes of student misbehavior, and she expects her students to help solve problems.

In each of these classrooms, the teacher's ideas about self-control are firmly embedded in her personal beliefs about the types of social skills students need to learn. Teachers who hold a tight rein on student behavior, like Ms. Whitney, expect their students to obey and respect authority. Teachers who loosen the reins, like Ms. Loop, hope their students will learn to get along with others and be responsible for their own behavior. A student who blossoms in Ms. Loop's class might chafe at the tight control in Ms. Whitney's classroom, and that student can become a discipline problem.

The variety of teacher opinions about the purpose of discipline underscores the fuzziness that surrounds the meaning of self-control. It is ironic to note that with all the attention educators give to reading, writing, mathematics, and other academic subjects, rarely is the hidden curriculum of self-control examined. From the time they first step inside their own classrooms, teachers are largely left to their own devices to determine what self-control skills they will foster. The unspoken norm in most schools is that as long as teachers maintain control of their classrooms, they are on their own.

The subjective veil that obscures the hidden curriculum of self-control was first pierced by Fritz Redl and David Wineman in their classic study of aggressive youth, *Children Who Hate* (1951). Like neurosurgeons who map the topography of the brain by studying brain-injured individuals, Redl and Wineman plotted the behavioral underpinnings of self-control by studying the actions of troubled youths in crisis. Through systematic observation of juvenile delinquents in a residential program—Pioneer House—Redl and Wineman discovered that, rather than being a single-faceted characteristic that a student either has or does not have, self-control is a general term for a series of specific social skills that young people develop as they mature and learn to cope with the hurdles of daily life. Figure 1.2 lists the social skills that Redl and Wineman identified as constituting self-control.

Redl and Wineman found that several different types of stressful events or situations precede a breakdown in self-control. Some youngsters stand up to the challenge and maintain self-control; others are overcome by negative feelings and lash out verbally or physically without regard for consequences.

Figure 1.2: REDL AND WINEMAN MODEL OF SELF-CONTROL

Self-Control Skills

- Tolerate frustration
- Recall personal contributions to conflict
- Maintain composure during unstructured activities
- Use previously satisfying experiences as resources
- Distinguish between subjective and objective time
- Assess feelings of others
- Learn from personal experience
- Participate in competitive games and activities

- Use materials appropriately
- Take care of possessions
- Accept affection and gratification
- Are realistic about rules and routines
- Anticipate consequences
- Evaluate group norms
- Learn from others' experience
- Cope with success
- Manage group pressure
- Cope with mistakes and failure
- Select alternative ways of getting along with others

Experiences That Trigger Loss of Self-Control

- Anxiety, insecurity, or fear
- Unfamiliar situations or experiences
- Reminders of traumatic experiences

- Group excitability
- Open or unstructured space
- Guilt

Consider an 11-year-old who is looking forward to a family trek in a nearby state park. A downpour begins just as the family prepares to leave, and the trip is canceled. The frustration generated by such a disappointment is obvious, but our young hiker regroups by calling a friend to come over and play. It is easy to overlook the smooth functioning of this 11-year-old's ability to tolerate frustration. The anatomy of self-control becomes apparent only when the mechanism breaks down. It certainly is not difficult to imagine a different reaction in a young man who has not learned how to cope with frustration.

In their research, Redl and Wineman highlighted the interactional nature of self-control. Simply stated, Redl and Wineman found that behavior is a function of the student interacting with the environment. It is as important to identify environmental situations that trigger the loss of self-control (for example, a canceled trip) as it is to understand a student's self-control abilities (for example, managing frustration).

An understanding of the precursors to a breakdown of self-control helps teachers to anticipate classroom disruptions. Awareness of events or situations that trigger loss of self-control in students provides the teacher with valuable information for intervening before a youngster causes a classroom disturbance. A proactive, rather than reactive, approach to managing troubled youngsters is the foundation of the Self-Control Curriculum.

Self-control is the ability to maintain composure when confronted with a challenging situation. Judging a student's behavior as impulsive identifies only half the problem. It is necessary to go one step further and describe the type of situation or incident that triggers impulsivity in an individual student. Strong feelings such as resentment or such everyday events as walking into a noisy assembly hall may be all it takes to send a disruptive youngster into a behavioral tailspin.

There is a great deal of variability in the makeup of each young person's self-control abilities. For example, some students can handle frustration, but they have difficulty with competition. Other children are models of decorum until a few students in the classroom are overstimulated and they get caught up in the excitement. (Redl and Wineman called this "group intoxication.") Teachers who identify individual patterns of self-control abilities are able to anticipate situations that trigger self-control breakdowns and intervene before a child loses control.

A SELF-CONTROL CURRICULUM

Educators are scurrying for solutions to violent and irresponsible behavior in the schools. The problem is serious, and the educational response runs the gamut from metal detectors to improving students' self-esteem. As practical and well-meaning as these ideas appear, they overshoot the mark. Before we can change the behavior of students, we need to examine our beliefs about how young people change and grow. Too many discipline practices sacrifice learning on the altar of obedience (Nichols, 1992). Students need the opportunity to take control of their own lives.

Redl and Wineman's model of self-control is usually overlooked by educators in their quest for effective discipline models. Many classroom-management practices emphasize how to get youngsters to behave, while neglecting the question of what skills need to be emphasized. Imagine trying to teach math, reading, science, or any other academic subject without such guidelines as texts, reading levels, or tests and you have an understanding of the impracticality of teaching self-control without a curriculum.

In order to develop a theoretically sound and practical social-skills curriculum for disruptive students, a group of elementary and secondary teachers and

I launched the Preventive Discipline Project (Henley, 1994). The purpose of this field-based research project was to develop a self-control curriculum including an inventory of student self-control abilities, self-control instructional objectives, and classroom activities to teach self-control. Using Redl and Wineman's model of self-control as a guide, my colleagues and I observed, documented, and analyzed behavioral outbursts of hundreds of troubled students in general and special education classrooms. Data was collected using both qualitative and quantitative measures, including anecdotal records, behavior frequency checklists, and behavior checklists developed from Redl and Wineman's model.

We had two criteria for developing a self-control curriculum. First, the identified social skills had to apply to a variety of classroom settings. This required consensus on behavioral expectations for students and recognition of the effect of teacher style on student behavior (Rezmierski, 1987). Second, the social skills needed to generalize to life outside of school. A social-skills curriculum is inadequate if it does not pinpoint the skills needed for success in the community as well as in school.

After 4 years of data collection, revisions, and animated discussions, we found that self-control consists of 20 specific social skills. We classified these into five domains: controlling impulses, following school routines, managing group situations, managing stress, and solving social problems (see Figure 1.3).

The Self-Control Curriculum is an antidote for school behavior problems. An antidote is a remedy, not a cure. It counteracts the effects of something toxic, but it does not remove the source of the poison. Teachers alone cannot solve the problems of disruptive youth; but, for the time each day that students are in school, teachers can help them learn more effective ways of getting along with themselves and others.

This book is designed with elementary and middle school teachers in mind. However, the Self-Control Curriculum and teaching practices are appropriate at the high school level as well. For example, cooperative learning, peer tutoring, brainstorming, and role-playing are useful tools for teaching self-control, regardless of age or subject area.

Some of the features of the Self-Control Curriculum are:

- Instructional methods for teaching self-control (see Chapter 3);

- Positive behavioral supports for handling disruptive actions and supporting self-control (see Chapter 4);

Figure 1.3: THE FIVE DOMAINS OF SELF-CONTROL

Control Impulses

- Manage Situational Lure
- Demonstrate Patience
- Verbalize Feelings
- Resist Tempting Objects

Manage Group Situations

- Maintain Composure
- Appraise Peer Pressure
- Participate in Group Activities
- Understand How Behavior Affects Others

Solve Social Problems

- Focus on the Present
- Learn From Past Experience
- Anticipate Consequences
- Resolve Conflicts

Follow School Routines

- Follow Rules
- Organize School Materials
- Accept Evaluative Comments
- Make Classroom Transitions

Manage Stress

- Adapt to New Situations
- Cope With Competition
- Tolerate Frustration
- Select Tension-Reducing Activities

- A research-based, social-skills curriculum including goals, objectives, and activities for merging self-control instruction with academics (see Chapters 5–10);

- The Self-Control Inventory (SCI), a standardized, curriculum-based rating form for identifying student self-control strengths and weaknesses (see Appendix A); and

- The Self-Control Curriculum Student Self-Report Form in English and Spanish (see Appendix B) and the Family Report Form (see Appendix C).

EMPOWERING YOUNG PEOPLE

No one has described more articulately the need for students to have some control of their lives than William Glasser (1993). To change their behavior, students need opportunities to make choices and take responsibility for their decisions. In describing what he calls "Control Theory," Glasser points out that control of one's life is encoded in the human psyche as firmly as the need for survival and love. The need for control finds fruition in self-direction. But making good choices in life, Glasser maintains, requires practice and encouragement. When adults who work with disruptive young people provide them with opportunities to take responsibility for themselves and others, the results are encouraging.

A quality shared by many successful youth programs is an emphasis on empowering students. Before troubled youngsters can become contributing members of society, they first must believe that they are capable of reshaping their lives.

It is easy to talk about change, but not so easy to make personal change happen. Change is difficult and requires free choice. Change cannot be dictated. A frontal assault filled with imperatives about how another person "should be" is bound to be greeted with resistance and resentment.

Changing destructive thought patterns, changing bad habits, and changing ways of dealing with other people requires commitment and opportunities to learn from mistakes. We cannot expect students to change if they feel they have no control over their own lives. Without hope, there is no future.

Alfie Kohn (1993) has written extensively on student self-determination. He points out five benefits of empowering students:

1. A student's general sense of well-being is improved. Feeling in control of one's life enhances both physical and mental health.

2. To learn to be responsible, a student must have the opportunity to make choices and learn from both successes and failures.

3. Student choice enhances both motivation and achievement.

4. Collaborating and sharing power with students is interesting, fun, and challenging.

5. Empowerment communicates respect.

If providing students with choices has so many beneficial aspects, why don't more teachers do it? Why is there still, particularly in educational programs for students with chronic behavior problems, such a predominant reliance on controlling students?

There are several reasons why teachers resort to authoritarian tactics when confronted with disruptive student behavior:

- Some teachers have a need to control. It is part of their personalities, and, of course, it carries over into their teaching.

- Some colleges and universities overlook classroom management in their teacher-preparation programs.

- Classroom management may be given short shrift in teacher-preparation programs, but it takes center stage in the schools. Young teachers quickly learn that they will be judged first and foremost on how they are able to control their class. This "sink or swim" approach to classroom management curtails taking risks and experimenting.

- Some teachers harbor secret fears about their students. They are afraid that if they give up control in the classroom, the students will run wild.

- Many teachers want to give their students more responsibility, but they do not know how to go about it.

When teachers try democratic ways of working with their students, the results can be enlightening. Consider the following statement by AnnMarie Samble (1992), an experienced teacher who decided it was time to try something different:

> *The first 2 years I taught students with emotional problems, I spent endless hours refining and implementing a point system that gave consequences for inappropriate behavior and positive reinforcement for appropriate behavior. In my mind, a well-behaved class meant that the teacher was in charge and that the children would learn. What I forgot to ask myself was—in charge of what? After re-examining my system, I realized I was indeed in charge—I was in charge of counting, tallying, recording, adding to, and taking away points! Points that had little or no meaning to the lives of my students. I thought that the children were learning from this system, that they were gaining knowledge from this experience. What I failed to recognize is the children had become non-active participants in changing their own behavior.*

One of the first things Samble changed was her method of establishing classroom rules.

A positive way to increase compliance with rules is to teach students the social skills necessary to function together. We developed our classroom rules together as a group. I led the students in a discussion about their responsibilities. We talked about what is expected of them and about particular discipline problems we might encounter. From this discussion we made a list of rules, and we determined consequences for broken rules.

Samble's transition from controlling to democratic teacher highlights a point that is often misunderstood. Empowering students does not mean relinquishing adult authority. It is a sharing, rather than an abdication, of power. Teaching and learning is a mutual activity. By helping your students learn to make decisions, you will give them the tools they need to succeed in life. Behavior change cannot be dictated. However, it can be negotiated.

HOW TO USE THIS BOOK

This book is a practical guide for teaching self-control to elementary and middle school students. However, the curriculum, teaching strategies, behavioral supports, and assessment forms are easily adapted to the high school level. The Self-Control Curriculum is appropriate for both special and general education students. The emphasis is educational. You can teach self-control skills using many of the same teaching methods used for academic subjects, including cooperative learning, brainstorming, and peer tutoring. Many of the suggested instructional strategies merge self-control skill development with academics. Children's literature, social studies, language arts, and even math and science can be used to teach self-control.

Chapter 2 introduces the Self-Control Inventory (SCI), which is located in Appendix A. In this chapter, you will learn how to use the SCI to identify student self-control strengths and weaknesses. Your rating of individual students will provide a framework for selecting specific self-control goals and objectives for individuals or for your entire class.

The Student Self-Report Form in Appendix B and the Family Report Form in Appendix C will provide you with additional information about how students view themselves and how families view their children. You will find that sharing perceptions is a powerful tool for change.

Chapter 3 details several methods for teaching self-control. The emphasis is on instructional methods that empower students. Included in this chapter are cooperative learning, peer tutoring, role-playing, brainstorming, children's literature, and student-centered activities.

Chapter 4 describes specific positive behavioral supports that reinforce self-control. Both nonverbal and verbal interventions are described in this chapter. Each support has a proven record of success in handling disruptive behavior. Preventive discipline strategies are highlighted.

Chapter 5 provides an overview of the Self-Control Curriculum model. It spells out guidelines for utilizing the sample activities in Chapters 6 through 10.

Chapters 6 through 10 detail goals, objectives, sample activities, and behavioral supports matched to each self-control skill. Each unit begins by showing you how to introduce a specific self-control skill to your students. Each self-control skill is divided into component subskills. Students need opportunities to discuss and practice social skills across the curriculum. Thus, each self-control subskill is matched to typical classroom activities. Besides planned lessons, self-control instruction is also a moment-to-moment occurrence in classrooms. Behavioral supports that best encourage each self-control skill are identified and briefly explained.

Chapter 11 emphasizes the resiliency of young people. Both research and daily experience support the notion that children are capable of overcoming difficult lives. We can never predict which young person will make it and which will not. Therefore, our responsibility is to give each child our best effort.

The forms and checklists in the Appendices can be reproduced and used as needed.

SUMMARY

Disruptive youth have an invisible disability. They are handicapped by their lack of self-control. Their hard lives have taught them all the wrong lessons for achieving their goals. It is critical to reach these young people early in their schooling in order to help them learn the social skills they need for success in later life.

Many teachers already practice self-control curriculum strategies. They allow students choices; they encourage students to solve their own problems; they foster activity-centered learning. What the Self-Control Curriculum has to offer these teachers is direction in the specific skills that constitute self-control. The Self-Control Curriculum delineates the social skills necessary for success both in school and society at large. The assessment procedure outlined in the next chapter lays the foundation for teaching self-control by providing a systematic method for pinpointing students' self-control strengths and weaknesses.

REFERENCES

Browning, K., & Loeber, R. (1999). Highlights from findings from the Pittsburgh Youth Study. *Office of Juvenile Justice and Delinquency Prevention Fact Sheet #95.* Rockville, MD: Juvenile Justice Clearinghouse.

Federal Interagency Forum on Child and Family Statistics (1999). *America's children: Key national indicators of well-being.* Washington, DC: Author. Retrieved January 9, 2003, from http://www.childstats.gov/americaschildren/

Glasser, W. (1993). *The quality school teacher.* New York: Harper Perennial.

Goleman, D. (1995). *Emotional intelligence.* New York: Bantam Books.

Henley, M. (1994). A self-control curriculum for troubled youngsters. *Journal of Emotional and Behavioral Problems, 3*(1), 40–46.

Henley, M., & Long, N. (1999). Teaching emotional intelligence to impulsive-aggressive youth. *Reclaiming Children and Youth: Journal of Emotional and Behavioral Problems. 7*(4), 224–229.

Kohn, A. (1993). *Punished by rewards: The trouble with gold stars, incentive plans, A's, praise, and other bribes.* New York: Houghton Mifflin.

Lewis, B. L. (1992). Do conduct disordered gang members think differently? *The Journal of Emotional and Behavioral Problems, 1*(1), 17–20.

New York University Child Study Center (2001). *A month of mental health facts: Fact-of-the-day.* New York: Author. Retrieved January 9, 2003, from http://www.aboutourkids.org/articles/mhfacts.html

Nichols, P. (1992). The curriculum of control: Twelve reasons for it; Some arguments against it. *Beyond Behavior, 3*(2), 5–11.

Redl, F., & Wineman, D. (1951). *Children who hate.* New York: Free Press.

Rezmierski, V. E. (1987). Discipline: Neither the steel nor the velvet, but the maturity inside the glove, that makes the difference. *The Pointer, 31*(4), 5–13.

Samble, A. (1992). From points to prevention. Unpublished manuscript.

Shoda, Y., Mischel, W., & Peake, P. K. (1990). Predicting adolescent cognitive and self-regulatory competencies from preschool delay of gratification. *Developmental Psychology, 26*(6), 978–986.

U.S. Department of Education. (1998). *Twentieth Annual Report to Congress on the Implementation of the Individuals with Disabilities Education Act.* Washington, DC: U.S Government Printing Office.

U.S. Public Health Service (2000). *Report of the Surgeon General's Conference on Children's Mental Health: A national action agenda.* Washington, DC: Department of Health and Human Services. Retrieved January 9, 2003, from http://www.surgeongeneral.gov/topics/cmh/childreport.htm

Way, D. (1993). I just have a half heart. *Journal of Emotional and Behavioral Problems, 2*(1), 4–5.

Self-Control Inventory 2

During the past 30 years, I have visited and talked with hundreds of teachers about their students, and I have heard the same lament over and over: "Don't tell me what's wrong with this student. Tell me how I can teach her." Their search reminds me of my first job when I was fresh out of graduate school. I was hired to teach a class of students who were labeled behavior-disordered and emotionally disturbed.

I was eager to meet the school's psychological advisor, Dr. Knowles. I anticipated that he would have a lot of useful suggestions for developing a therapeutic classroom environment. After welcoming me to the school, Dr. Knowles began to talk about my students in a slow, thoughtful cadence:

"Bruce," he began, "is obsessive-compulsive, most likely brought on by anal-retentive tendencies nurtured by his elderly parents."

"On the other hand, Stan," he continued, "is hyperactive; his 135 IQ indicates he is much more capable than his present school performance shows. His constant chatter is anxiety-based, and this has caused him a lot of difficulties."

"Now, let's move on to Janie. This youngster is paranoid; she has an active fantasy life; and she is, of course, delusional in much of her thinking. According to her Bender-Gestalt score, her problem may be organically based."

As I listened to his descriptions, I began to do some fantasizing of my own. What was I going to do with these obsessive-compulsive, organically damaged, hyperactive kids? The more we discussed the psychological labeling of my students, the more ill-prepared I felt.

My students were evaluated, analyzed, and dissected into neat psychological categories; however, there was nothing in the reams of psychological evaluations that gave me the slightest clue about how to teach my class. That is the purpose of this book. It is a practical guide for teaching students with disruptive behaviors.

This chapter provides an overview of how to use the Self-Control Inventory (SCI), a curriculum-based rating scale that provides a comprehensive assessment of student self-control abilities.

Curriculum-based assessment determines the learning needs of a student, based on the student's performance compared to the curriculum. A teacher selects a specific curriculum in science, math, reading, or any other subject and determines the skills and concepts to be taught. Typically, curricula are arranged in terms of goals, which in turn are subdivided into specific objectives. For example, a math goal for fourth grade might be multiplying by two-digit numbers. Objectives for this goal would include multiplying by multiples of ten, multiplying with two-digit factors, and word problems. By defining the curriculum and skills to be taught in such a specific manner, a teacher can observe students solving problems, give periodic quizzes, and collect samples of work to determine how well each student has mastered the curriculum.

THE SELF-CONTROL INVENTORY

I have applied the principles of curriculum-based assessment to the Self-Control Curriculum. Appendix A contains the Self-Control Inventory (SCI). The SCI is matched to the Self-Control Curriculum and is organized into five goal areas: impulse control, school routines, group situations, stress management, and social problem solving. The four self-control skills listed under each goal are explained, an example of each skill is provided, and a sample behavioral objective is included.

Appendix E describes the standardization of the SCI.

It takes 15 to 20 minutes to do an SCI rating. The classroom teacher, school adjustment counselor, or school psychologist can rate a student with the SCI.

Before filling out the SCI, the rater should be familiar with the student for at least 2 months. Ratings are based on a student's behavior compared to his or her peers. Reliability is enhanced when two raters, both of whom know the student well, do independent ratings and compare results.

The rating system is as follows:

1. Student *rarely* demonstrates ability (persistent and frequent self-control problems).

2. Student *sometimes* demonstrates ability (self-control problems are exhibited on a regular basis).

3. Student *often* demonstrates ability (only occasionally demonstrates lack of self-control).

4. Student demonstrates *mastery* (behavior is appropriate for age).

5. N/A (item not applicable).

6. N/O (item not observable).

Lowest-rated items identify priorities to teaching self-control skills.

Ratings from the Self-Control Inventory can be used in the following ways:

- To identify student self-control abilities.

- As a guide for determining priorities for teaching self-control (Chapter 3).

- To anticipate situations that trigger self-control problems and to identify appropriate positive behavior supports (Chapter 4).

- To write behavior-management and individual education plans (IEPs) (Chapter 5).

- To establish priorities for inclusion programs.

THE STUDENT SELF-REPORT FORM

How many times have you heard the following student excuses: "It wasn't my fault." "I didn't do anything." "Why are you picking on me?" Student perceptions of their own behavior frequently are at odds with the teacher's view. The purpose of the Student Self-Report Form (Appendix B) is to provide a means for students to rate their own self-control abilities. The ratings provide teachers and students with a concrete procedure for comparing perceptions of behavior.

The rating system uses a system of statements that are rated. The Student Self-Report Form is written in plain and simple language. A Spanish version also appears in Appendix B.

There are several benefits to using the Student Self-Report Form.

- Each statement requires the student to reflect on his or her behavior. Thinking about one's behavior is a critical first step to changing one's behavior.

- Analysis of the student rating provides an opportunity for discussing student behavior without criticism.

- The results of the Student Self-Report Form can be used as a basis for developing a student-teacher behavior contract. More details about behavior contracts appear in Chapter 4.

- After completing the Student Self-Report Form, students have a clearer idea about the self-control skills on which they need to work.

- Students can monitor their own progress after instruction in self-control skills.

Including students in evaluating their classroom behavior highlights personal responsibility for their actions. Sharing perceptions about student behavior paves the way for working together to promote the acquisition of self-control skills.

THE FAMILY REPORT FORM

One of the best predictors of a student's school success is family participation. When a young person has deficits in social-skill development, family involvement in the school program is critical. The Family Report Form (Appendix C) provides families with the opportunity to compare views with teachers about a student's behavior. A Spanish version of the form also appears in Appendix C. Several benefits of including family members in this assessment process are listed below.

- Family input can confirm that specific self-control skills are needed at home, as well as at school.

- Families can reinforce the development of targeted skills.

- Teacher-family conferences are improved because of a shared perspective about a student's behavior.

- The Family Report Form can help educate parents about desirable social skills.

- The Family Report Form identifies strengths as well as weaknesses in self-control.

Used in combination with the Self-Control Inventory, the Student Self-Report Form and Family Report Form provide a comprehensive assessment package for promoting self-control skills at school and home.

LINKING ASSESSMENT TO INSTRUCTION

Teachers of students who present problems with behavior will find the Self-Control Inventory a useful tool for guiding instruction in self-control. After rating a student with the Self-Control Inventory, the teacher can target specific self-control skills for classroom instruction. For example, Mr. Jones gave Martin B., a sixth-grader, a rating of 1 (rarely demonstrates ability) on skill #14, *copes with competition*. Using this information to prioritize Martin's self-control needs, Mr. Jones structured some of Martin's classroom activities to help him learn to manage the stress that accompanies competition. Mr. Jones planned cooperative learning activities in order to provide Martin with opportunities to succeed by working with others, rather than competing against them. Success through cooperation would later be used as a basis for exposure to gradual doses of competition.

Students with chronic behavior problems will exhibit a constellation of self-control strengths and weaknesses. By identifying both skills and shortcomings, the Self-Control Inventory helps build on existing social skills to broaden a student's self-control abilities.

Alex, a fifth-grader, has mastered self-control skill #14, *copes with competition*, but he sometimes demonstrates difficulty with self-control skill #20, *resolves conflicts*. His teacher selected Alex as referee during recess. The experience of mediating games between other students placed Alex in a familiar situation where he could use an existing skill as a basis for learning a needed self-control skill.

A sample problem-solving tool for developing classroom educational strategies from the Self-Control Inventory is the Behavior Management Plan (BMP) included in Appendix D. Also included in Appendix D for your use is a blank BMP outline. The following two chapters detail teaching and behavior management strategies that can be used for developing Behavior Management Plans.

Chapter 3 provides the background you will need to plan self-control lessons. Specific teaching practices, such as role-playing, cooperative learning, and peer tutoring support self-control development by capitalizing on students' resourcefulness.

Teaching Self-Control 3

Whatever we learn to do, we learn by actually doing it: men come to be builders, for instance, by building, and harp players, by playing the harp. In the same way, by doing self-controlled acts, we come to be self-controlled; and by doing brave acts, we become brave.

—William Bennett (1993), *The Book of Virtues*

I learned my most valuable lesson about teaching self-control as a full-time substitute teacher in an urban elementary school. Each morning, I walked to the teachers' lounge to wait for the school secretary to tell me in which classroom I would be subbing that day. I had approximately 20 minutes over a cup of coffee to make my plans and evaluate the kind of situation I would encounter. My substitute-teacher position gave me a unique view on how teachers' classroom-management practices influenced student self-control.

After a few months of comparing how students behaved in different classrooms, I made a discovery. The classrooms that were the most docile and controlled when the teacher was present were the most difficult substitute assignments. Like smoldering volcanoes, these classes would erupt with disruptions when the teacher was absent.

Mr. Abbot's classroom stands out most clearly in my memory. The students, about 27 of them, greeted my entrance with what can be described only as pure glee. (The refrain, "Oh boy, a sub," is well known to anyone who has been a substitute teacher.) From the moment I set foot inside the door, I was confronted with one disturbance after another. Michael complained because I wouldn't let him go to the library. Ashley wanted to play records. James ran over to the window to sail paper plates he found in the supply closet. Jesse picked a fight with Alan. The disruptions were contagious, and I spent the day hopelessly battling the epidemic with meager threats and bribes.

During my first weeks, I assumed that the wild student behavior was just part of the package that went along with teaching at a school attended by poor, streetwise kids. However, I soon got a pleasant surprise. Not all class-rooms launched out of control on my arrival. In Mr. Torrey's classroom, I encountered few problems. Students showed me where the pass was, pointed out the learning center schedule, and helped me get organized. Their instructional time was structured by "learning center" activities. Several tables were placed around the perimeter of the room. Each center was clearly labeled with a sign on the wall: "art," "math," "science," "writing," and "language development." Each learning center was stacked with gear. The math table, for instance, had a balance scale, rulers, pencils, and many small objects to be weighed and counted. Three students at a time worked at each of the tables. They helped each other, compared calculations, and moved to an empty space at another table when they were done.

In one corner of the room, there was a comfortable reading area. An old couch, big floppy cushions, and a bright orange rug invited each student to curl up with any one of the hundreds of children's books stacked neatly in adjacent bookcases. Soft classical music served as a soothing counterpoint to the busy learners.

Mr. Torrey often referred to his classroom as a "community of learners." He encouraged students to take responsibility for their learning through weekly contracts in which each student wrote down his or her learning priorities for the following week.

After a few months, I began to see a distinction between teachers of class-rooms that were chaotic, such as Mr. Abbot's, and classrooms such as Mr. Torrey's, where students maintained their composure when the teacher was absent. Chaotic classrooms were quiet and compliant in the presence of the teacher. These teachers talked about students needing consistency, and they emphasized the importance of clear limits with punishment for disruptive behavior. The desks in these classrooms tended to be set in rows, and much of the day's business was directed by the teacher from the front of the room.

On the other hand, classrooms that kept their composure when I subbed were beehives of activity. The teachers favored learning centers, group discussions, and students working together in small groups. Mr. Torrey wanted his students to be responsible for their own behavior. He was proud of the fact that he could step outside of the classroom or even go for a short errand down the hall and his students would barely notice that he was gone.

Over time, I came to see that the absence of the teacher with the concomitant arrival of a substitute teacher was a litmus test to evaluate the effectiveness of a classroom-management system. I began to understand that students need to learn how to control their behavior without the presence of a looming authority figure. I learned that a teacher cannot lecture a student about responsibility. Students need opportunities to evaluate situations and to learn from their mistakes.

An all-too-common response to the irresponsible behaviors exhibited by disruptive students is to focus teacher and administrative resources on repressing students through such punitive measures as detention, suspensions, and homespun behavior-modification programs. At best, such control practices keep students glued to their seats in cheerless classrooms that prohibit natural urges that accompany learning such as spontaneity, movement, and animated conversation.

Jane Knitzer, Zina Steinberg, and Brahm Fleisch completed one of the most comprehensive surveys of educational programs for students with behavior problems ever undertaken. In their report, *At the Schoolhouse Door* (1990), the authors lament the lack of classroom possibilities afforded students to learn how to get along with others. In their site visits, Knitzer and her colleagues found that students who lacked social skills were not allowed to socialize. They found academic underachievers so bored with copying notes off the blackboard that they slept at their desks. They discovered a plethora of behavior-modification techniques, such as point and level systems designed with the single intention of getting students to complete unimaginative learning tasks. Most of all, they report mechanical adherence to rigid discipline policies. Consider the following description from their study:

> *In a middle school self-contained classroom in a southern state, we observed a rigid point system that included giving children "sentences" for negative behavior. The rules were that a child lost 100 points for hitting another child; 200 points for talking back to a teacher. During our visit, one of the children explained to us that it was possible to "erase" the sentence, either by writing a real sentence 50 times, or by reciting the Gettysburg address, although our particular informant had no idea who wrote the Gettysburg address and for what purpose.* (p. 26)

The noted Swiss psychologist Jean Piaget said that children construct their own knowledge. Learning requires trial and error, activity, and opportunities to compare perceptions with others. Dictated learning is an oxymoron. The centerpiece of a classroom that teaches self-control is interesting things to do. William Morse, who has spent a lifetime encouraging educators to respect the complexity of personal growth in the education of disruptive students, said:

If school is not inviting, if the tasks are not clear, interesting, and at an appropriate level, how can we expect pupils to stay on task? Adverse student reactions should be expected when classes are dull, teaching is uninspired, and failure is built in. (1987, p. 6)

When the teacher controls the classroom, the learning assignments given to students are likely to include a great deal of paper-and-pencil work. Basal texts will proliferate. Worksheets and workbooks are the tools of passive learning and compliance. In such an atmosphere, the joy of learning is stifled.

Many students need help in learning to control their anger, their frustrations, and their behavior. This is best achieved in an atmosphere that fosters independent thinking, personal responsibility, and decision making to empower young people.

PROMOTING SELF-CONTROL IN THE CLASSROOM

Teachers promote the development of self-control abilities by providing classroom lessons that encourage participation and success. The following qualities are a synopsis of effective teaching practices that emphasize self-control development while providing students with engaging learning opportunities:

- *Make the lesson interactive.* Small groups that exhibit a balance of student social skills work best. This means paying attention to group dynamics to ensure that the shortcomings of one student are offset by the strengths of other students.

- *Personalize the activity.* High-interest activities work best. Students are most engaged with activities they can connect to on a personal level. Find ways to blend students' daily experiences into the curriculum.

- *Empower students.* Allow students to make decisions within an activity. This enhances participation and promotes personal responsibility. Powerlessness produces apathy; self-determination increases motivation.

- *Include a helping component.* Encouraging students to help each other is an affirmative teaching method for building self-control. Helping moves students beyond the egocentric thinking that underlies many self-control problems (for example, inability to verbalize feelings, inadequate conflict-resolution skills). Arrange activities that encourage sharing, listening, empathy, cooperation, and group problem-solving.

One or more of the four teaching processes outlined above can be incorporated into any lesson or activity. Some examples of teaching methods that include interaction, personalizing, empowerment, and helping are cooperative learning, peer and cross-age tutoring, children's literature, role-playing, activity-centered learning, and brainstorming. Each of these approaches is student-centered. Each empowers students and provides opportunities to learn self-control by highlighting personal responsibility for learning.

COOPERATIVE LEARNING

Cooperative learning enhances motivation by giving students control over their learning. Cooperative learning highlights several self-control skills, including *participating in group activities, coping with competition, resolving conflicts, organizing school materials,* and *learning from past experience.* Cooperative learning can be used to teach any part of the curriculum—from mathematics to story writing. It has a strong research base and is frequently used in public-school classrooms. Cooperative groups should be selected carefully to ensure a heterogeneous balance between males and females, high and low achievers, and students with different social skills. Students will need instruction about how to work together.

Roy Smith (1987), a junior high school teacher, found that his students were conditioned to lean on the teacher for guidance because of a steady diet of teacher-directed instruction. He outlined the following steps for teaching cooperative skills:

- Identify the specific skills group members will need to demonstrate, such as listening, providing information, and giving feedback. Brainstorm with students about behaviors that help move groups along and behaviors that inhibit group work.

- Highlight the need for cooperative skills. Keep in mind that doing individual work and competing for grades are commonplace in school and that it may take some time for students to understand the value of cooperation.

- Review the value of cooperative skills in a variety of situations both in and out of school.

- Practice cooperative skills throughout the day.

- Arrange opportunities for students to discuss their use of cooperative group skills.

The most common method for organizing cooperative groups is called the jigsaw approach. Each student is assigned a specific responsibility within the group. Like putting together a jigsaw puzzle, the group work is not completed until each piece is in place. For instance, a group assignment could be a report on drugs. Each student's "piece" could be a different source of information, such as a medical reference book, newspaper clippings, magazine articles, and an encyclopedia. Avoid building competition—such as pitting one group against another—into cooperative group performance.

PEER AND CROSS-AGE TUTORING

One of the best ways to learn something is to teach it to someone else. Peer and cross-age tutoring places the student squarely in the center of the teaching-learning process. It encourages personal responsibility for learning and is highly motivational when used with at-risk, disabled, and slow learners. Peer tutoring and cross-age tutoring help to develop several self-control skills, including the ability to *learn from past experience, anticipate consequences, organize school materials, demonstrate patience, verbalize feelings, accept evaluative comments,* and *describe the effect of behavior on others.*

While there is no one best treatment for behavior problems in the classroom, giving students responsibility does enhance self-confidence and improve behavior. Disruptive students are usually the last to be selected for special consideration and the first to be deprived of pleasant experiences. Peer and cross-age tutoring gives students a sense of purpose and control over time spent in school.

Consider this question posed by William Glasser, the architect of control theory: Why is it that no one needs to prompt or goad students who participate in such extracurricular projects as school newspapers, science clubs, and debate clubs? The answer, he says, is that extracurricular activities provide students with opportunities to direct their own actions (Gough, 1987). Students feel ownership for their projects, and consequently they are motivated to work hard and succeed.

Peer and cross-age tutoring provides the same intrinsic incentives as do extracurricular activities. Tutoring puts students in the role of teacher. Students help others and contribute to the school community.

The following six steps are useful when establishing a peer or cross-age tutoring program:

1. Start small. Begin with pairs of four or five students. Slow development of a tutoring program helps work out the kinks. Having older students tutor younger students is a good way to begin, because it sidesteps problems in group dynamics that may contribute to discipline problems in a classroom.

2. Prepare the school for a tutoring program. A written proposal outlining scheduling and monitoring procedures will ensure that each person is certain of his or her role in the program.

3. Determine a tutoring schedule. Daily 30-minute sessions produce the best tutoring results.

4. Inform parents about the program. Invite parents to school to observe the program in action.

5. Train tutors. Outline the content to be covered and highlight the interpersonal skills needed to be an effective tutor.

6. Hold weekly feedback sessions with tutors. Encourage them to discuss ideas that work and problem areas. Have weekly meetings with tutees to learn how effectively the program is working for them.

CHILDREN'S LITERATURE

The notion of teaching social skills through literature is not new to American education. In the early part of the last century, such basal texts as *McGuffey's Eclectic Reader* were the mainstay of reading instruction.

Within the past decade, educators have recognized that children's literature can play an integral part in teaching both the skill and enjoyment of reading. Children's literature helps shape students' views on life in many ways. Themes that exemplify the self-control curriculum, such as *anticipating consequences, learning from past experience,* and *resolving conflicts,* permeate children's literature.

Reading aloud from a book in class and discussing how the characters are reacting to their situation highlight social-skills development. Some ways of using children's literature include:

- Explore themes in stories. Ask students to identify similar situations in their own lives.

- Stop reading and ask students what they would do in the place of the main character or ask students what they think will happen next.

- Have students rewrite the conclusion to a story.

- Ask students how they felt about the story.

- Ask students about parts of the story they would like to change.

Follow-up activities, such as writing a group story or having students write stories about when they have faced a similar situation, help students to understand how self-control skills are a part of everyday life. Figure 3.1 lists titles from children's literature with themes that match the self-control curriculum. Additional titles are included in the sample units.

Figure 3.1: CHILDREN'S LITERATURE

Primary Level

Self-Control Skill	Title	Author	Publisher
Following rules	*No Jumping on the Bed*	Tedd Arnold	Dial
Learning from past experience	*Where the Wild Things Are*	Maurice Sendak	Scholastic
Anticipating consequences	*Just a Dream*	Chris Van Allsburg	Houghton Mifflin
	Brother Eagle, Sister Sky	Susan Jeffers	Dial
Adapting to new situations	*Letting Swift River Go*	Jane Yolen & Barbara Cooney	Trumpet Club
	A Mouse to Be Free	Joyce Warren & Jerry Lang	Sea Cliff
Managing situational lure	*No David*	David Shannon	Scholastic
	Easy Does It: The Tale of Excitable Sam	Margaret Hopkins	Scholastic
Demonstrating patience	*Moose, Of Course*	Lynne Plourde	Down East Books
	Take Turns Penguin	Jeanne Willis	Carolrhoda Books
Understand how behavior affects others	*Uncle Willie and the Soup Kitchen*	Dyanne Disalvo-Ryan	Mulberry Books
Verbalizing feelings	*The Oceans of Emotions*	Nicole Clark	PremaNations Publishing
	Chrysanthemum	Kevin Henkes	Greenwillow
	Wemberly Worried	Kevin Henkes	Greenwillow
	Do Animals Have Feelings Too?	David Rice	Dawn Publishing
Resisting tempting objects	*Junie B. Jones Is Not a Crook*	Barbara Park	Random House
	Sarah, Plain and Tall	Patricia MacLachlan	Harper Trophy
	The Legend of Bluebonnet	Tomi dePaola	Penguin Putnam Books for Young Readers

Figure 3.1: CHILDREN'S LITERATURE (continued)

Elementary Level

Self-Control Skill	Title	Author	Publisher
Verbalizing feelings	*The Polar Express*	Chris Van Allsburg	Houghton Mifflin
Resolving conflicts	*The Stronghold*	Mary Hunter	Harper & Row
Tolerating frustration	*The Phantom Tollbooth*	Norton Juster	Random House
Managing situational lure	*The Dragon's Boy*	Jane Yolen	Harper & Row
	There's a Boy in the Girls' Bathroom	Louis Sachar	Random House
Demonstrating patience	*Learning to Slow Down and Pay Attention: A Book for Kids About ADD*	Kathleen Nadeau & Ellen Dixon	Magination Press
	Being in Control: Natural Techniques for Increasing Your Potential for Success in School	Jason Alster	Magination Press
Resolving conflicts	*Somewhere Today: A Book of Peace*	Shelly Moore Thomas	Albert Whitman and Co.
Verbalizing feelings	*The Janitor's Boy*	Andrew Clements	Simon & Schuster
To resist tempting objects	*Esperanza Rising*	Pam Muñoz Ryan	Scholastic Trade
	The Worst-Case Scenario Survival Handbook	Joshua Piven & David Borgenicht	Chronicle Books

ROLE-PLAYING

During a role play, students respond spontaneously to situations created by the teacher. This encourages students to look at a situation from another person's point of view. It encourages empathy, and it helps students to shed their egocentric view of life. Role-playing has been around for a long time, and it is a powerful tool for learning.

Role-playing adds zest to virtually any school activity. Favorite children's stories can be re-enacted with different endings. Historical figures and events can be replayed. Students can role-play other people. They can even role-play objects, such as a bolt of electricity or blood coursing through an artery.

All children are natural role-players. They do it all the time in their play. Role-playing capitalizes on student imagination and spontaneity.

One of my favorite role-playing scenarios was the "magic peddler." I walked into my classroom hunched over with a hat draped over my eyes. Over my shoulder I carried a sack, which contained a number of articles of clothing: the friendship belt, the tie of disappointment, the anger cap, the security sweater, and so on. I bartered my magic goods for a story. Each student had to tell me why he or she deserved a specific item. Their stories often were surprising and moving. I was amazed at how easily my students talked about their feelings when they were pretending. It was a powerful activity; and at the conclusion, I was fascinated with how easily students with emotional problems took to role-playing.

The following are tips for getting started with role-playing:

- Begin with warm-up sessions to encourage spontaneity. Use situations that are free of stereotypes, such as role-playing a tree, a snowflake, the number two, or a vocabulary word.

- Do not criticize or comment; this stifles creativity. The same limit on comments applies to students; accept all interpretations.

- When students ask several questions about details in the scene, they are resistant to spontaneity.

Because role-playing has the potential for unlocking deep-set feelings, it should be introduced gradually into classroom activities. Start with exercises that do not contain personal matter and see how students respond. As you move into role plays that reflect self-control skills, monitor how students react. Too much personal identification with a role play may shame a youngster. Be certain in your role-playing that you provide ample time to discuss student feelings generated by the simulation.

LEARNING CENTERS

Activity-centered learning is the best behavior-management tool available to teachers. I know this is a strong statement, but consider that the major causes of discipline problems are boredom, apathy, goofing off, and just plain wasting time. All of these problems are solved when students are busy. There is little to inspire a student in worksheets, listening to droning lectures, and taking turns reading from textbooks.

Consider these research findings from the U.S. Department of Education monograph, *What Works: Research About Teaching and Learning* (1986):

- *How much time students are actively engaged in learning contributes strongly to their achievement.* (p. 34)

- *Numerous studies of mathematics achievement at different grade levels show that children benefit when real objects are used as aids in learning mathematics. Teachers call these objects "manipulatives."* (p. 29)

- *Children learn science best when they are able to do experiments, so they can witness "science in action."* (p. 23)

- *The most effective way to teach writing is to teach it as a process of brainstorming, composing, revising, and editing.* (p. 27)

Each of these statements supports a simple but powerful principle of learning: Students learn best when they are doing something. If schools were not constrained by the 2-by-4 curriculum (ceiling, floor, and four walls of the classroom), passive learning would be the exception, rather than the rule. The trick is to figure out ways to keep learning active even though both teachers and students are constrained by the physical limitations of school buildings.

One of the best ways for teachers to inject vitality into their classrooms and lessons is through learning centers. Acquire a few rectangular tables; place them on the perimeter of the classroom. Hang a sign above each saying "math center," "science center," or "arts and crafts center," and you are on your way to an activity-centered classroom. Learning centers reduce boredom by allowing students to move from one learning activity to another. Locating concrete learning materials that will work for your classroom will take most of your time. Figure 3.2 lists a starter kit of materials for your classroom learning centers.

The emphasis on independent learning and concrete experience offered by learning centers provides a framework for the following self-control skills: *demonstrating patience, organizing school materials, following rules, making classroom transitions, maintaining composure, adapting to new situations, tolerating frustration,* and *selecting tension-reducing activities.* These skills develop as students move about the room, taking turns at each learning center and working together.

For instance, learning centers support making classroom transitions. The concrete learning materials help students manage frustration and reduce tension. The engaging appeal of learning centers helps students maintain composure even while other students are being disruptive.

Tasks to be completed at each learning center usually are indicated by a sign that lists the steps to follow. This helps students organize themselves and stay on task. Activity-centered learning that is promoted through learning centers encourages students to experiment, to question, and to describe their own unique perceptions.

Figure 3.2: LEARNING CENTER STARTER'S KIT

These materials can be reused many times for various activities.

Math Learning Center

- stopwatch
- rulers
- carpenter's tape measure
- several tailor tape measures
- geoboards
- yardstick
- graph paper
- recipes
- Cuisenaire rods (or equivalent)
- dominoes
- bathroom scale
- colored pencils
- string
- balance scale
- small objects to count and weigh

Science Learning Center

- metronome
- stethoscope
- microscope (a good one)
- slides
- eyedroppers
- directional compass
- egg coloring dyes
- petri dishes
- galvanic skin response meter
- batteries
- copper wire
- small lightbulbs
- pond water
- cups and beakers
- reference books

Writing Learning Center

- tape recorder
- Polaroid-type camera
- stationery
- magazines
- scissors
- computer for word processing and printer
- pens and pencils

Arts and Crafts Learning Center

- glue
- construction paper
- scissors
- white paper
- tracing paper
- crayons
- pencils
- pieces of felt and other materials that can be glued on paper
- leather and cloth scraps
- needle and thread
- pipe cleaners
- rulers
- magic markers
- colored pencils
- art books

BRAINSTORMING

Most classroom instruction takes place in large groups of 15 or more students. This large group situation is ideal for using brainstorming as a teaching tool. Brainstorming provides both teacher and students with a structured method for developing creative ideas.

A brainstorming session is guided by the teacher or a student who typically stands before the group at a blackboard to write down group ideas. Overhead projectors or paper on an easel are other common means of recording brainstorming sessions.

Brainstorming helps students think because it capitalizes on both analysis and intuition. There are no right or wrong answers in brainstorming. This may take some getting used to by students who are conditioned to give only the "right" answer. Figure 3.3 outlines rules for brainstorming.

Brainstorming is a good method for running class meetings. The problem or issue is presented to the class, and students feel free to offer solutions. The fundamental rule of brainstorming—Do not prejudge ideas—encourages and supports taking risks.

Figure 3.3: RULES FOR BRAINSTORMING

1. Say anything that comes to mind.

2. Don't judge your ideas or the ideas of others.

3. Don't limit your ideas by trying to have them make sense. Allow yourself to say whatever comes to mind.

4. Let your thoughts come quickly. Let them flow.

5. Remember that people use only a small part of their brain. Brainstorming enables you to unlock the parts you don't ordinarily use. Surprise yourself with new ideas.

6. See how many creative ideas and solutions you can come up with, and don't restrict your thoughts in any way.

7. Be outrageous and have fun!

Adapted from "Creative Brainstorming" in *Learning the Skills of Peacemaking,* by Naomi Drew (Jalmar Press, 1987).

During a typical brainstorming session, students present ideas in rapid-fire sequence. Such self-control skills as *conflict resolution, learning from past experience, accepting evaluative comments,* and *participating in group activities* are developed through brainstorming sessions. For example, the brainstorm leader (either teacher or student) poses the question, "How can we raise money for a class field trip?" Conflicting ideas are accepted during the brainstorming session, and all ideas are listed. Then the class members discuss the relative merits of each idea. The review of suggestions strengthens skills in accepting evaluative comments, because the winnowing of ideas results in some ideas being accepted while others are rejected. Many suggestions will be based on past experience; and, because brainstorming is fun, a high level of group participation is assured.

AN INSTRUCTIONAL MODEL FOR TEACHING SELF-CONTROL

Each of the teaching methods discussed above incorporates the four basic elements of teaching self-control: empowerment, helping others, active learning, and personalizing the curriculum.

Students who lack self-control act out their social problems all day long. Teachers need a social-skills program that covers all the contingencies of a normal school day. Each academic subject offers multiple opportunities for teaching the Self-Control Curriculum. Teachers can incorporate the Self-Control Curriculum into their daily lessons by using a two-phase instructional model:

Phase I introduces a specific self-control skill. You teach the concept by introducing the self-control skill and providing students with an enjoyable activity that helps them understand the vocabulary, the meaning, and the usefulness of each skill.

Phase II demonstrates how to merge the self-control subskills into the curriculum. Also included in Phase II are positive behavior supports that support the development of each self-control skill.

In Phase I, the emphasis is on the cognitive understanding of a specific self-control skill. It is a process of re-educating students about their behavior. The reason many young people have social-skill deficits is that they have not been taught the social skill. Such skills as verbalizing feelings, learning from past experience, and anticipating consequences do not develop without support. Young people learn these social skills as they mature and develop in nurturing environments, both in the family and the community. The absence of self-control skills signals the need to first introduce or reacquaint young people with the specific skill.

Phase II of self-control instruction weaves self-control abilities into the general curriculum. Social skills can be taught and learned in the same manner as any other subject. A teacher begins a lesson on fractions by introducing students to the concept of fractions and then presenting students with learning experiences that require the use of fractions. The same routine is followed in the Self-Control Curriculum. Each skill is divided into two or three subskills. Matched to each subskill are sample teaching activities. This model is not inclusive, but it is intended to demonstrate how self-control social skills can become a part of the daily teaching routine.

Phase II also describes positive behavior interventions that support each skill. Teaching self-control is a moment-to-moment activity. Spontaneous opportunities to model self-control skills, coach students on the use of self-control skills, and remind students of the need to maintain self-control are numerous in every classroom. Positive behavior interventions that support self-control are described in detail in the next chapter.

To summarize, the Self-Control Curriculum is an educational program designed to teach self-control to disruptive students. Assessment information gleaned from the Self-Control Inventory, along with the Student Self-Report and Family Report Forms, provides you with the information you need to determine the specific self-control skills your students need to learn. Sample units in chapters 6–10 outline the two-phase instructional model for merging self-control instruction into the daily schedule. Chapter 5 describes in detail how to arrange Phase I and Phase II activities and positive behavioral supports.

REFERENCES

Drew, N. (1987). *Learning the skills of peacemaking.* Carson, CA: Jalmar Press.

Gough, P. (1987). The key to improving schools: An interview with William Glasser. *Phi Delta Kappan, 68*(9), 62–65.

Knitzer, J., Steinberg, Z., & Fleisch, B. (1990). *At the schoolhouse door: An examination of programs and policies for children with behavioral and emotional problems.* New York: Bank Street College of Education.

Morse, W. (1987). Introduction: An ounce of prevention? *Teaching Exceptional Children, 19*(4), 4–6.

Smith, R. (1987). A teacher's view on cooperative learning. *Phi Delta Kappan, 68*(9), 663–666.

U.S. Department of Education (1986). *What works: Research about teaching and learning.* Washington, DC.

Positive Behavioral Supports

4

People must never be humiliated—that is the main thing.

— Anton Chekov

Classroom management is the essential teaching skill. Teachers cannot teach and students cannot learn in a disruptive classroom. The Self-Control Curriculum provides a framework for anticipating student behavior problems and intervening before the student becomes disruptive.

Too much classroom time is wasted dealing with discipline problems after a disruptive incident has occurred, and not enough time is given to supporting self-control before a problem arises. Such self-control skills as patience, verbalizing feelings, organizing school materials, and making classroom transitions can be encouraged through a variety of teacher supports. Positive behavioral supports are spontaneous teacher actions that reduce discipline problems.

Consider the following scenario:

> *Amber, a sixth-grader with a reputation for aggressiveness, refused to finish her work. She felt slighted because she raised her hand to ask for help, but her teacher, Mrs. Reilly, was preoccupied with some other students. Amber reacted by crumpling her worksheet and throwing it on the floor. Simultaneously, Amber announced to the entire class that she was "fed up with freaking math." Her disruptive behavior led to the following dialogue:*
>
> *Mrs. Reilly: "Amber, pick up that paper and put it back on your desk."*
>
> *Amber: "Pick it up yourself. I'm sick of this trash work."*

The entire class is on alert, a fact that is clearly embedded in Mrs. Reilly's mind. At this point, student and teacher are engaged in a conflict, and Mrs. Reilly is confronted with a dilemma. If she ignores Amber, Mrs. Reilly fears that the other students will perceive her as weak, someone who is easily pushed around. On the other hand, if she comes down hard on Amber, she risks escalating the conflict. Mrs. Reilly is stuck in a situation that could have been prevented.

If Mrs. Reilly had completed an SCI rating on Amber, she would have discovered that Amber had difficulty with skill #15, *tolerates frustration*. This information would have enabled Mrs. Reilly to anticipate Amber's frustration. Forewarned that Amber is easily frustrated, Mrs. Reilly could intervene to help Amber manage her frustration. Such interventions include allowing Amber to work with another student, periodically checking on Amber's progress, and decreasing the number of math problems Amber needs to solve. Mrs. Reilly could have practiced preventive discipline.

PREVENTIVE DISCIPLINE

Prior knowledge of situations that strain a student's ability to maintain self-control allows the classroom teacher to intervene before a student loses self-control, rather than after a disruptive incident. Prevention also allows the teacher and student to work together to develop specific self-control skills.

In much the same way that a track coach helps an athlete learn to negotiate hurdles before racing in competition, the teacher can plan supports to help a student learn to cope with specific challenges to self-control. For instance, a student who demonstrates difficulty with skill #13, *adapts to new situations*, is an ideal candidate for showing a new student around the school and introducing the newcomer to students and teachers. Support through role reversal provides the student with insights for changing his or her own behavior.

Supports must be targeted at the cause of the disruptive behavior, not the behavior itself. Two students may be engaged in the same disruptive behavior for different reasons; an intervention that was successful with a student on Monday might not work on Tuesday. Successful classroom management requires that teachers be flexible in handling discipline problems. Think of classroom supports as tools in a teacher's kit. The more tools you have at your disposal, the more effective you will be at your work. As you review the following supports, check those supports you do not normally use. Then make a conscious effort to add them to your repertoire.

NONVERBAL SUPPORTS

Nonverbal behavior supports are preferred to verbal supports because they do not interrupt classroom activities. All of the following nonverbal supports can prevent a student's behavior from creating a classroom disturbance.

Proximity

Moving about the room while teaching keeps students alert. Avoid "frontal teaching," that is, teaching while rooted to the front of the classroom.

Planned ignoring

Many minor classroom disruptions can be ignored. Remember, no teacher can expect to have 100% student attention all the time. Do not distract yourself and your students by attending to minor sounds or movements. Without attention, in many instances the disruptive behavior will cease.

Eye contact

You do not need an "evil eye," but looking directly at a student emphasizes that you know what is going on.

Signal interference

Sometimes all it takes is a finger to the lips or a palm turned downward to signal that a particular behavior should cease.

Body language

Erect posture and confident carriage indicate leadership. Lack of confidence and lethargy are suggested by slouching, lack of vigor, and frowning.

Removal of seductive objects

Paper clips, pencils, wadded pieces of paper, and small toys can be distracting. Remove the object and return it at the end of the day. However, keep in mind that "manipulatives" are excellent teaching tools. Discriminate between distracting objects and objects that help students learn more effectively.

Modeling

Teach by example. Demonstrate the type of behaviors you want to see in your students. Students size up teachers. They may not know how to describe your behavior beyond "nice" or "mean," but they are aware of how you treat them and other adults.

VERBAL SUPPORTS

Teacher-student talk helps clarify expectations. Be brief and to the point.

Alerting

Giving students 10-minute, 5-minute, and 1-minute warnings about the termination of an activity helps support smooth transitions from one activity to another.

Humor

Many potential teacher-student power struggles can be defused by a light-hearted comment. Pay attention to children's humor, and you will see that you do not need to be a comedian to make them laugh. Be careful not to be sarcastic or to say something that could be construed as making fun of someone.

I once overheard a teacher say to a student, "When you refuse to finish your work, it makes my bald spot turn red." The student laughed; the teacher asked her to give the math another try; and the problem was defused.

Hypodermic affection

Give the student a shot of caring. This can be very effective if delivered at a time it is least expected. For instance, when a student is misbehaving, the teacher responds with a compliment about her new haircut. Unexpected affection can defuse a young person's anger and break the tension.

Show personal interest

Provide as many strong indicators as possible that you respect your students for who they are, not for what they do. Encourage them to talk about their lives, and share stories about yourself. A trusting relationship between teacher and student is the cornerstone for building self-control.

Accept and acknowledge student feelings

Do not make the common mistake of accepting only good feelings. Anger, sadness, frustration, and disappointment are all part of the human experience, and all these feelings should be allowed and respected. It is not feelings but how students mismanage their feelings that can cause them problems.

Negotiate

Students take responsibility for their behavior when they have some ownership of the rules and sanctions. Work out issues together through class discussions. You are striving to teach students how to make good choices; so provide some latitude for mistakes, and allow students to learn from natural consequences.

A word of caution: Do not forget that you are the adult and leader. Be clear about what is open to negotiation and what is not.

"Withitness"

"Withitness" means knowing what is going on around the classroom at all times. A "withit" teacher can be providing individual help or working with a small group but still be aware of what other students are doing.

Restructuring

Sometimes even the best lesson misses the mark. Whatever the reason, do not take student disinterest personally; simply switch gears and move to something else. Rather than wasting time harping at students to "pay attention," change the activity.

Praise

Too much praise creates a dependency on adult approval; too little praise indicates that you do not care. Be honest in appraising students, and keep in mind that it is effort, rather than final product, that is most praiseworthy.

Positive reinforcement

Positive reinforcement is a behavior-modification technique that uses rewards to motivate students. The use of positive reinforcement is common practice in schools. Grades, rewards, and contests with prizes are time-honored practices that encourage student effort.

Naturally occurring consequences are the best reinforcers. For example, the feeling of success after completing a research project or the enjoyment found in reading a good book provide intrinsic positive reinforcement that strengthens the behaviors of researching and reading. Students need positive outcomes, and some students need the teacher to provide positive reinforcement in order to be motivated.

Many young people, particularly primary school children, enjoy stickers and other tangible rewards for work. Tangible reinforcers, such as stickers, tokens, and point systems, work best when there is a clear need for an external structure to help youngsters stay focused. Recent criticism about the misuse of reward systems built on positive reinforcement should remind educators that reward systems can be overdone.

In his book, *Punished by Rewards: The Trouble with Gold Stars, Incentive Plans, A's, Praise, and Other Bribes* (1993), Alfie Kohn points out several pitfalls of using contrived rewards to motivate students. Some of his criticisms include:

- Rewards punish because some people do not get the rewards they feel they deserve.

- Rewards rupture relationships by pitting students against each other in competition for the goodies.

- Rewards ignore reasons by disregarding the causes of behavioral troubles.

- Rewards discourage risk-taking because when we work for a reward, we do exactly what is necessary and no more.

Intermittent reinforcement

Intermittent reinforcement is a reward that surprises. The randomness of the intermittent reinforcement adds to the novelty and pleasure. A pizza party for hard work or a movie on a Friday afternoon for good behavior remind students that perseverance pays off.

Rehearsal/coaching

Many successful social-skills programs use rehearsal or coaching techniques to teach new social behaviors. The teacher outlines the specific steps needed to successfully use a social skill, and takes the student through the process one step at a time.

Usually, the teacher models a target behavior. This is followed by a learning activity, such as role-playing, that illustrates the skill in action. Students are provided with feedback about their performance in the role play and are encouraged to do homework assignments and classroom activities that review the skill.

Behavior contracts

A behavior contract is a signed agreement between a teacher and student stipulating a specific behavior the student will work to achieve. Some of the information in a behavior contract includes a clear description of target behavior, a reward for achieving the behavior, when and where the behavior will occur, and signatures by both teacher and student.

Behavior contracts are effective tools for reinforcing student responsibility because behaviors are clearly delineated, the student agrees to the contract, and the signatures indicate that the contract is an official agreement. A sample behavior contract is illustrated in Figure 4.1.

"I" messages

It is important for students to communicate their feelings. Likewise, it is important for teachers to model verbalizing feelings. Authentic communication requires personal ownership of feelings. Teachers model direct expression of feelings through "I" messages. Such statements as "I am frustrated" or "I am angry" are appropriate expressions of feelings. "I" messages do not attack students' characters by blaming students. Thus, it is inappropriate to use such statements as "You think only of yourself" or "It's your fault that I'm in a bad mood."

Reality appraisal

Students often act without considering the consequences of their behavior. Reality appraisal reminds students that for every action there is a reaction. When students forget their homework, they might have to do it over again. Getting into a fight can lead to suspension.

Reality appraisal is a direct appeal to a young person to weigh disturbing behavior against the possible outcomes.

CORRECTIVE BEHAVIORAL SUPPORTS

Corrective supports are actions taken in reaction to a student disruption. However, it should be kept in mind that strong teacher feelings, such as anger or impatience, can contribute to discipline problems. The Conflict Cycle (Figure 4.2) depicts how stress can generate student feelings that lead to disruptive actions. Adult or peer response can create more stress and more disruptive behavior.

You can avoid the conflict cycle by not taking student misbehavior personally. Corrective behavioral supports require teachers to respond coolly, with professional detachment. The corrective interventions that follow help to support self-control by communicating respect while also clearly spelling out classroom limits.

Sane messages

Haim Ginott, a noted expert on classroom management, used the term "sane messages" (1971) for clarifying expectations for classroom behavior. Address the disruptive situation, not the student's character. Describe the behavior you want to stop and the behavior you want to see the student exhibit. Avoid an angry response.

Figure 4.1: STUDENT BEHAVIOR CONTRACT

Name _____ Date _____

School _____ Class _____

_____ agrees to work on the following
self-control skills:

_____

_____

_____

I agree to try my best.

Student signature: _____

Teacher signature: _____

Family member signature: _____

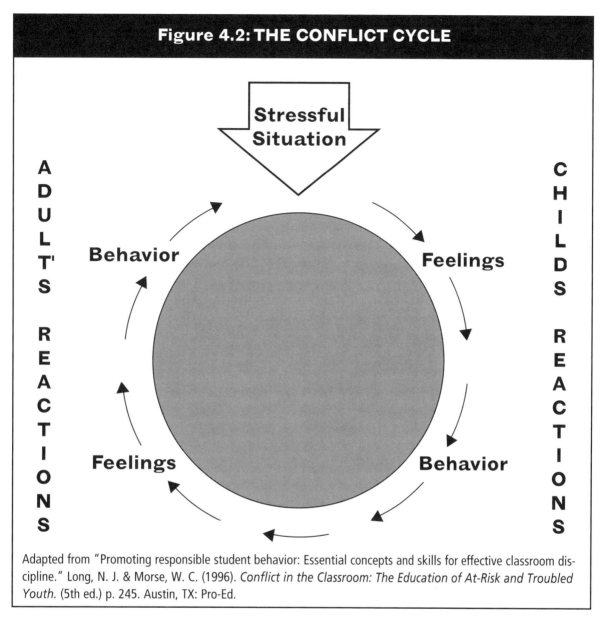

Figure 4.2: THE CONFLICT CYCLE

Stressful Situation

ADULTS' REACTIONS

CHILDS REACTIONS

Behavior

Feelings

Feelings

Behavior

Adapted from "Promoting responsible student behavior: Essential concepts and skills for effective classroom discipline." Long, N. J. & Morse, W. C. (1996). *Conflict in the Classroom: The Education of At-Risk and Troubled Youth.* (5th ed.) p. 245. Austin, TX: Pro-Ed.

For example, two students are goofing off in the back of the classroom during a class activity. A sane message is: "Lin and Maria, concentrate on your work. Your talking is disrupting other students' concentration."

Ginott contrasted sane and insane messages. An insane message applied to the same situation attacks a student's character. For instance, "Cut it out, you two. You are always creating a nuisance." This message compels through shame. It might get immediate results, but it has bought obedience at the price of the students' self-respect (Ginott, 1971).

Direct appeal

Be candid. Tell students about the behaviors you find troubling and why they bother you. We all have our pet peeves, personal limits, and bad days—

adults as well as students. Do not hesitate to simply point out that a certain behavior is irritating or frustrating. By talking about your feelings, you are helping your students learn about their ability to affect other people's emotions.

Logical consequences

The sanction should match the offense. Logical consequences work best when students have played a role in deliberating about sanctions for violation of classroom rules. Keep in mind that the consequences need to seem logical to the students, as well as to the teacher. If you spill paint, the logical consequence is that you clean it up. If you get into a fight during recess, the logical consequence is that you lose recess for a predetermined number of days. To make the best use of logical consequences, give students leeway to settle their own disputes.

Never punish in anger, and do not take misbehavior personally. If students perceive that consequences are fair, they will respond favorably.

Threats

Threats are most effective when used sparingly. You do not need a cannon to swat a fly, and you do not need threats to stop every classroom disturbance. Observe a teacher who often uses threats and you will see both an unhappy teacher and a resentful group of students.

Remember, when you threaten a student, you must follow through.

Time-out

The practice of removing a disruptive student from the rest of the group is a time-honored practice that is easily abused. In the early days of public schools, students were placed in the "dunce's corner." When I was a student, a few of the teachers in my school made troublesome students stand in the wastepaper basket while holding all their textbooks. The intention of time-out is not to shame, but to give students time to cool off and reflect on their behavior.

After 5 or 10 minutes, the sanction effect wears off; and, for some young people, time-out can inadvertently reinforce disruptive behavior. Time-out should be initiated directly after a disruptive incident. Because offending students miss classroom instruction, time-out should be used judiciously and each use should be recorded. Document the student's name, date, description of the episode, in/out time, and type of time-out. Also describe the student's behavior during time-out.

If you find yourself resorting to time-out frequently with the same student, then the intervention is not working and it should be reviewed.

Time-out is an ideal opportunity for talking with students about their behavior, using the technique of Life Space Intervention.

Life Space Intervention

In their book, *Life Space Intervention: Talking with Children and Youth in Crisis* (1991), Mary Wood and Nicholas Long outline how to use a crisis situation to teach self-control. Life Space Intervention (LSI) is an ideal verbal intervention to use during time-out. It is a six-step procedure for getting students to take responsibility for their behavior. Consult Wood and Long's book for a thorough explanation.

The following is a summary of the six LSI steps:

1. Focus on the incident. Convey support and understanding. Get the student talking about the incident. Clarify strong feelings in a nonjudgmental fashion.

2. Help the student to reconstruct the scene. A timeline identifying specific events should be established. You are gathering data about the student's perception.

3. Find the central issue and select a therapeutic goal. Determine what student feelings or perceptions are contributing to the problem. (Note: Use the Self-Control Curriculum to identify outcomes.)

4. Choose a solution that the student values as beneficial. Encourage the student to take ownership for the solution. If he or she does not do this, select a solution around group values and reality consequences.

5. Plan for success. Discuss typical problem situations and how the solution proposed in Step 4 will be implemented.

6. Get ready to resume activity. Plan for the student's transition back into the ongoing activity.

Used in combination with the Self-Control Inventory rating, the above teacher interventions support student self-control by helping students through difficult parts of their day. The emphasis is on preventing discipline problems by anticipating challenges to student self-control and responding with teacher interventions that help students maintain their composure.

PUNISHMENT

Some teachers confuse compliance with self-control. They strive for obedience. They think that if they use a mixture of rewards and punishments, their students will learn to behave themselves. When students comply, they are rewarded; transgressions are punished. These teachers are looking for quick fixes for behavior problems.

A pervasive stereotype in public schools is that students get into trouble because they have not been punished for previous misdeeds. On the contrary, the life histories of many students who exhibit behaviors are replete with cases of overzealous punishment.

Serious misbehavior cannot be ignored. When used judiciously, punishment clarifies limits and establishes consequences for specific behaviors. On the other hand, punishment does not teach new behaviors. If used frequently or harshly, punishment only hardens a young person's resistance to change. B.F. Skinner, the reluctant guru to many punishment-oriented behavior change programs, stated:

> *What's wrong with punishments is that they work immediately; but give no long-term results. The responses to punishment are either the urge to escape, to counterattack, or a stubborn apathy. These are the bad effects you get in prisons, or schools, or wherever punishments are used.* (Goleman, 1987, p. C3)

Many young people need help in learning how to deal with their anger, despair, and frustrations. Punishment forces compliance, rather than encouraging students to take responsibility for their own behavior. Punishment is a big stick, and it works best when used occasionally. Routine use of punishment saps the teacher-student relationship, turning partners in learning into adversaries. I call this the Miss Clarisa effect.

Miss Clarisa was my fourth-grade teacher. She was young and inexperienced. Her basic tactic for dealing with misbehavior was to rise out of her seat in the front of the room, move ominously toward the offender, and begin listing all the bad things that would happen if she "had to come down there." Having Miss Clarisa approach your desk was terrifying. You never knew if she was going to shame you with verbal abuse or manhandle you.

She tormented one student in particular. Tony sat at a desk near the front of the room. When Miss Clarisa flew into a rage, it often was aimed at Tony. She would throw him out of his seat and pick up his desk, dumping all his books on the floor. Red-faced, she would scream at him to pick up his books and stand in the wastebasket in the corner holding all of them.

From the first day of school to the last, Miss Clarisa continued her search-and-destroy missions. We rarely experienced a peaceful day. You would think all of this fury would intimidate us, but it actually had the opposite effect. By October, her aggressive behavior had contributed to a state of steady alert among many of the boys. Our senses were sharpened, and we prided ourselves on being able to pick up the early-warning cues that Miss Clarisa was about to lose it. That is when the adversarial game between teacher and students began in earnest.

The basic plot was simple and is well known to basketball players. When two players foul each other, usually it is the second player who gets caught. A well-delivered paper clip was a good bet to get the receiver in trouble when he turned around to find his tormentor. Another favorite was the throat-clearing chorus. Pete cleared his throat. Ed cleared his throat a little louder; Miss Clarisa turned around from the blackboard. The air was heavy with expectation. We were walking a tightrope; who would fall off? Dick cleared his throat softly; Miss Clarisa continued to write. Doug cleared his throat, and she was on him like a tornado. During recess we would compare notes on who participated, who got caught, and the degree of wrath we were able to provoke from Miss Clarisa.

While the Miss Clarisa effect may seem remote and far-fetched in today's schools, it is not. Anger, hostility, and even physical punishment directed toward students occur more often then many of us would like to admit. Many states continue to uphold the right of teachers to "paddle" students, though it is sad to contemplate the effect of corporal punishment on a student who has been abused either physically or sexually. A few sensible guidelines can help ensure that punishment does not contribute to a student's problems.

- Develop rules and sanctions with students in order to encourage their ownership of classroom limits.

- After a punishment, discuss with the student new behaviors that would help avoid future punishments.

- Keep track of how often punishments are used. If the frequency of punishment is constant or increases (the Miss Clarisa effect), then the utility of the intervention should be reviewed.

- Logically connect the punishment to the infraction. (See the previous description of logical consequences.) Logical punishments work best when there has been some prior discussion and agreement among teacher and students, matching punishments with infractions.

- Do not confuse punishment with discipline. Punishment uses power to gain compliance. Discipline molds character.

Punishment is based on an oversimplified stimulus-response notion of human nature. Youngsters, particularly troubled youngsters, need more than punishments to turn around their complicated lives. They need compassion and opportunities to help others. They need success and the chance to learn from their failures. And most of all, they need someone to teach them the social skills they lack.

SUMMARY

Chapter 1 described the Self-Control Curriculum. Chapter 2 outlined the Self-Control Inventory and explained how it can be used to target self-control objectives for classroom instruction. Chapter 3 detailed specific types of instructional methods that teach self-control; and this chapter showed how classroom positive behavior supports can support self-control development.

The next six chapters explain in detail how to combine self-control objectives, classroom activities, and positive behavioral supports to teach the Self-Control Curriculum. Because teachers deal with groups of children, the activities are designed for use with an entire class or small groups of students. The activities and supports are suggested approaches to get the teacher moving in the right direction. Teachers should adapt the Self-Control Curriculum to meet their own needs.

REFERENCES

Ginott, H. (1971). *Teacher and child.* New York: Macmillan.

Goleman, D. (1987). Interview with B.F. Skinner. *New York Times,* August 25, 1987, C3.

Kohn, A. (1993). *Punished by rewards: The trouble with gold stars, incentive plans, A's, praise, and other bribes.* New York: Houghton Mifflin.

Long, N. J., & Morse, W. C. (1996). *Conflict in the classroom: The education of at-risk and troubled youth* (5th ed.). Austin, TX: Pro-Ed.

Wood, M. M., & Long, N. J. (1991). *Life space intervention: Talking with children and youth in crisis.* Austin, TX: Pro-Ed.

Introduction: Sample Units 5

The Self-Control Curriculum is an educational method for teaching students to think more clearly about themselves and the world around them. It is a cognitive model for improving behavior. Flawed thinking is at the core of self-control problems. Misperceptions, rationalizations, and lack of reflection undermine self-control development.

- Misperception—Monique is walking down the high school corridor between classes. She passes two students who are whispering and laughing. They look in her direction and turn around. Monique walks over and grabs the closest one by the collar. Monique is sure they are making fun of her and she vows to get even after school.

- Rationalization—On his way home from school, William passes a red sports car idling in front of a convenience store. He hops in the front seat and drives off. Two hours later, he is picked up by the local police. When they ask him why he stole the car he replies, "Hey, it's not my fault that the guy was so dumb he left the car running while he went in to get a loaf of bread. It's his fault I stole his car, not mine."

- Lack of reflection—Mateo returned to the alternative high school after a month in juvenile detention. He told the principal that he hated lock-up and would never go back again. Three days later, Mateo made lewd sexual remarks to a female student. He was suspended from school—a violation of his probation—and was sent back to juvenile detention.

The purpose of the Self-Control Curriculum is to teach students to consider reasonable alternatives before they act. The regular academic curriculum presents myriad opportunities to teach students the 20 core skills that make up self-control.

The following chapters present sample units for launching the Self-Control Curriculum. Each chapter provides examples for teaching the skills and subskills that make up self-control. These are samples, not scripted lessons. Eventually you will develop lessons to meet your own unique needs and the needs of your students. The sample lessons were developed with students from first to eighth grade in mind. However, once the system of integrating Phase I and Phase II lessons is clear, the curriculum can be adapted for older students. Keep in mind that when using the Self-Control Inventory to identify specific skills for instruction, student ratings should be based on comparisons with same-age peers.

Each chapter is a curriculum unit divided into two parts—Phase I activities and Phase II activities. Phase I introduces each self-control skill. Phase II merges each self-control skill with the academic curriculum. Within Phase II, each self-control skill is divided into sub-skills. For example, the first self-control skill is managing situational lure. This skill is divided into two sub-skills to identify appropriate behaviors outside the classroom and to adjust behavior to match the situation. Finally, each unit provides a list of positive behavior supports that encourage the development of each self-control skill.

PHASE I ACTIVITIES

The purpose of Phase I is to provide a basic understanding of the Self-Control vocabulary. One of the reasons students exhibit self-control difficulties is that they do not see the connection between their emotions and their actions. Emotions move us to action. The word "emotion" is derived from the French word "emou-voir" meaning "to stir up." Many young people are unaware that there are specific words for expressing an array of emotions. Inadequate emotional vocabularies limit a young person's ability to constructively deal with strong feelings. A student who does not understand the word "frustration" will be hard-pressed to identify her own feelings of frustration, much less make a sound decision about how to handle her frustration. Students who lack constructive avenues to express their feelings are bound to act those feelings out in non-constructive fashion.

The teacher's role throughout the Self-Control Curriculum is educational. Phase I lessons help students see how each skill presents itself in daily situations. What follows are some guidelines for moving beyond the samples and developing your own Phase I lessons.

- Present a stimulus to build student interest. Tell a personal anecdote, read a story from a newspaper or book, show a video segment, or present a role-playing scenario. Every good lesson needs a "hook" to grab student attention. Be enthusiastic. Encourage students to share related stories. Challenge students to come up with innovative descriptions of how they exhibit self-control in everyday life.

- De-personalize the lesson. No student should feel that the lesson is directed at him or her. Keep the discussion apart from recent classroom or school problems. If students suspect that your presentation is a veiled dictum on proper behavior, they will become defensive and ultimately lose interest.

- Connect the self-control skill to life outside of school. One of the major criticisms of social skill programs is a lack of generalization. Contrary to the dictums of some educational reformers, we do not teach reading and math to raise achievement test scores. We teach reading and math because these skills prepare students for life. Within this vein we also need to demonstrate to students that social skills are more than pathways to proper school decorum. Students with social skill deficits understand concepts best that are linked to concrete events and situations with which they are familiar. Phase I lessons should help students see the application of each self-control skill in their community and the world at large.

- Strive for student participation. Use brainstorming to build on student ideas. Use cooperative groups to get students thinking together. Follow up your introductory lesson with projects and themes. One group of elementary school teachers was concerned about teasing and bullying. They selected "how behavior affects others" as the skill they wanted to develop among their students. As a follow-up project to Phase I activities, they put up a bulletin board in the school lobby. It was titled "Good Deeds." When students witnessed an act of kindness among students, they pulled a colored index card from a folder on the bulletin board and jotted down a brief description. The cards were tacked to templates of flowers, animals, stars, and other designs. By the end of the month, the bulletin board had become a vivid public testimony to student kindness.

PHASE II ACTIVITIES

The academic curriculum presents myriad opportunities for teaching self-control skills. While Phase I activities introduce specific self-control skills, Phase II activities demonstrate for students how the self-control skill is manifested throughout their course of study. Through this process of immersion, the student comes to recognize how social skills have and continue to enhance our quality of life. There are no quick fixes here. Social skill development follows a lengthy and circuitous route.

While the standard curriculum is organized in a sequential step-by-step arrangement, the human brain organizes information in an idiosyncratic branching fashion. (Think spider web rather than ladder.) Direct instruction about how one should behave, or designated "social skill time" sessions, present information in fragmented bits. Meshing self-control skills with daily lessons helps students see the important role social skills play in the evolution of human culture. Consider the following examples:

- The self-control skill is appraising peer pressure. The Phrase II sub-skill is to act in accordance with personal beliefs.

- Social Studies—Do a unit on one or more individuals who helped change society through the courage of their convictions: Ruby Bridges, Jackie Robinson, Nathan Hale, Martin Luther King, Jr., Rosa Parks. Highlight cultural and gender differences and similarities. Research how these individuals grew up and the obstacles they had to overcome.

- Language Arts—Ask students to define the word "hero." Have students make a hero list. Emphasize that the list cannot include the names of celebrities. Bring in periodicals and have students analyze reports of regular people who engage in heroic acts. Have students brainstorm qualities of heroes. Have students write an essay on heroism in everyday life.

- The self-control skill is verbalizing feelings. The sub-skill is to identify feelings in others.

  - Social Studies—Ask the students to empathize with the people they are studying. For example: What feelings prompted the Boston Tea Party? Have a mock discussion among Boston Tea Party members the night before their raid. Address the following concerns: What will happen if we get caught? Is it worth the risk? Will our actions make a difference? Are our families in danger? How can we escape detection? What do we do next?

  - Language Arts—Use metaphors to encourage empathy in writing. Direct students to describe how it feels to be a washing machine, an old pair of roller skates, a neglected stuffed toy, a cube of sugar, or a bag of candy. Record responses on a tape recorder. Allow students to build on each other's ideas.

POSITIVE BEHAVIORAL SUPPORTS

Each Phase II unit is followed by a series of interventions that are useful supports for managing students' behavior. The matching of these positive behavioral supports to specific self-control skills—while not arbitrary—is an approximation. Every individual and situation is different. The wider the breadth of knowledge about positive supports the more options available to manage student behavior. Figure 5.1 lists research-based interventions and procedures that support student efforts to acquire self-control skills. Many of the listed interventions are self-explanatory; others are described in Chapter 4.

Figure 5.1: POSITIVE BEHAVIORAL SUPPORTS

Supports That Prevent Self-Control Problems

- Moving around the room
- Planned ignoring
- Signal interference
- Modeling
- Activity-based lessons
- Celebrating cultural diversity
- Communicating with families
- Allowing for student movement
- Providing organizational strategies
- Tolerating misbehavior symptoms
- Identifying antecedents that trigger behavior problems

- Identifying consequences that reinforce behavior problems
- Body language
- Eye contact
- Removing tempting objects
- Establishing smooth transitions between activities
- Promoting a sense of community in the classroom
- Giving students responsibilities
- Conducting regular classroom meetings
- Playing calm background music
- Linking instruction to student experience

Supports That Promote Emerging Self-Control Skills

- Humor
- Personal interest
- Alerting
- Encouraging effort
- Praise/incentives
- Negative reinforcement
- Rehearsing and coaching
- Reality appraisal

- Restitution
- Accepting and acknowledging feelings
- "Withitness"
- Restructuring
- Positive reinforcement
- Intermittent reinforcement
- "I" messages
- Direct appeal

Supports That Correct Self-Control Deficits

- Life Space Intervention
- Behavior contracts
- Time out
- Peer meditation

- Logical consequences
- Sane messages
- Natural consequences
- Punishment*

---

*Punishment is the presentation of a stimulus immediately after a behavior that decreases the future probability of the behavior. If the behavior does not decrease, punishment should be dismissed as a positive behavioral support.

Controlling Impulses 6

A key ability in impulse control is knowing the difference between feelings and actions.

— Daniel Goleman

Uncontained, impulsive behavior is a leading cause of discipline problems in today's schools. The thousands of students who are identified as having attention-deficit hyperactivity disorder (ADHD) each year are ample evidence that impetuous, impulsive behavior is a significant problem for many classroom teachers.

Redl and Wineman (1951) describe impulses as "the sum total of all urges, impulses, strivings, desires, needs, which seem to push in the direction of gratification, goal attainment, or expression. . . ." Impulses are powerful motivators to action. But rash, spontaneous behavior almost always leads to serious problems in school.

One of my students, 9-year-old Delores, was a bundle of impulses. She grabbed classroom materials without asking. She bolted out the door for recess. When upset, she climbed under tables, pulled desks over, and threw papers around the room. Her behavior angered other students and concerned school staff.

In September, one of my colleagues had requested that Delores be placed in his class. Four months later, he was in the school director's office saying that Delores had to go. The next day, the director asked me to come to her office for a chat. "Martin," she said, "would you consider taking Delores in your class?"

I did not need a lot of time to consider her request. I said, "Barbara, my class has really come along. Adding Delores at this time would upset the group harmony." However, I knew I had no choice. Our special education program was the last stop for troubled youngsters. After us, the only option was residential placement. None of us, teachers or administrators, wanted to see Delores shipped off to a residential program.

"I believe your classroom would be ideal," Barbara continued. "If anybody can work with her, you can." So I inherited Delores. She was my reward for doing a good job.

I accepted Delores with one stipulation: that I be given a small space outside the classroom where I could bring Delores as soon as trouble started. My plan was to use the space for time-out. I believed that immediate removal, along with a Life Space Intervention, would minimize her disruptions in the classroom and would give me the chance to teach Delores that there were consequences for her impulsive actions.

It was a rough road, but after 2 months, Delores showed significant improvement in impulse control. She was more patient, she used words instead of actions to express herself, and she resisted the temptation to grab at every object within reach.

Students like Delores need time and re-education to change. There is no shortcut to impulse control.

RE-EDUCATION

Re-education means teaching students the self-control skills they lack. Students demonstrate serious deficits in self-control for four reasons:

1. They come from chaotic home environments, and they have not been taught socially acceptable behaviors.

2. They know how they are supposed to behave, but they have not had enough opportunities to practice those behaviors.

3. They have an emotional or metabolic impairment that makes it difficult to direct their actions in acceptable ways.

4. Any combination of the above.

Each of these factors is amenable to re-education. Students need to be taught the social skills in which they have deficits, and they need practice in developing their self-control.

The first step in re-education is to identify the appropriate self-control skills for classroom instruction. In our research in the Preventive Discipline Project, we found that impulsive young people showed deficits in one or more of the following four self-control abilities: *managing situational lure, demonstrating patience, verbalizing feelings,* and *resisting the urge to hoard, manipulate, or handle tempting objects.*

MANAGING SITUATIONAL LURE

Space has an allure that impulsive youngsters find difficult to resist. Open spaces invite running. Enclosed spaces invite yelling. Field trips present constant challenges to impulsive students and their teachers. Students who experience difficulties managing situational lure can create havoc inside and outside the classroom.

Arlene was 8 years old, hyperactive, and showed discipline problems outside the structured space of the classroom. One day the staff at my school decided that the gymnasium would be a welcome relief to classroom quarantine for recess during inclement weather. The first rainy day, the five teachers in our special education program marched our 40 students into the cavernous gymnasium for games. The students were elated to be out of the classroom, and the teachers organized them into games.

Arlene was one of the last to enter. When she walked through the gymnasium door, she let out a whoop and started running. She dodged and weaved her way around pursuing staff with the agility of a halfback. By the time we corralled her, she had knocked over several of the smaller students and agitated practically everybody in the room, children as well as adults.

Arlene was so overstimulated that I had to take her back to the classroom, where we both spent the rest of the recess. With better preparation and support, Arlene was able to participate successfully in our rainy day gym recesses. If I had recognized that the gymnasium presented a situational lure to Arlene, the entire unfortunate scene could have been avoided. I could have prepared her for the gymnasium by discussing the situation with her beforehand and closely monitoring her entrance into an organized small-group activity. Her outburst was a reminder that impulsive students are subject to situational lure. We resolved not to handicap her in the future with poor preparation for spatial changes that were obvious challenges to her weak impulse control.

DEMONSTRATING PATIENCE

Approximately 25 young people and 1 adult populate the average elementary classroom. This uneven distribution of adult resources means that at any given time, as many as 24 children have to wait. They wait to take turns; they wait for help; they wait to perform. Waiting is as much a part of the daily classroom experience as reading, calculating, and lunch.

When students are able to contain their impulses and wait, no one notices, because this is expected behavior. When students are unable to wait—when they push in line, when they bother other students, when they yell out answers—everybody notices. Students who lack patience disrupt their own learning and everyone else's as well.

Patience is an acquired trait. All of us, adults and children, have times when we have to remind ourselves to be patient. Practicing patience, like physical exercise, builds stronger stamina and resolve to be patient. We know enough about the behavioral characteristics of impulsive youngsters to expect difficulties with patience. It should come as no great surprise that young people who have difficulties controlling their impulses also will have difficulty with patience.

Students who lack patience need more than rules to help them control their behavior. Rules prescribe, but they do not cure. Many classroom activities offer possibilities for teaching patience. Peer tutoring, cooperative learning, abbreviated assignments (for example, fewer problems on a math sheet), shorter lessons (that is, 15 to 20 minutes), and learning centers indirectly develop patience by putting less strain on weak attending skills while providing successful classroom experiences.

Direct instruction of patience is facilitated when the student recognizes the need to learn patience. Self-monitoring strategies are one way of helping a student take personal responsibility for change. Just as stepping on a scale helps an overweight person "own" his or her weight problem, a student counting the number of times he or she blurts out an answer provides concrete data that more patience is needed. Games that require listening, waiting, and taking turns can teach children to wait while still providing the instant gratification that many impatient youngsters need. Rehearsal strategies in which students repeat the steps needed to complete a problem, first aloud and then silently, help develop patience by breaking a task down into manageable steps.

Teaching patience either indirectly or directly is a better use of a teacher's time than incessant warnings or corrections that will continue all year and that do little more than highlight a student's inadequacies.

VERBALIZING FEELINGS

Many children who exhibit disruptive behaviors act rather than talk. They fight rather than negotiate. It is easier for them to run away from a problem than it is to explain their situation. They are limited by a lack of insight into their feelings and the feelings of others. Part of their problem is vocabulary; they are unaware that there are myriad ways of expressing feelings. Consequently, they are prone to oversimplify their feelings.

A limited understanding of the power of feelings and a propensity toward aggressive behavior is a formula for disaster in classrooms. The problem is compounded by home and community settings that reinforce the notion that hitting someone in the face is the best way to keep one's self-respect.

Re-education of these youths begins with a feeling vocabulary. Helping students link their internal experiences to the appropriate words provides a new way of expressing themselves. For street-wise students, it is important to present role models who articulate feelings and who show respect for the feelings of others. Ex-gang members, for example, can be influential in helping young people to see that words can be more powerful than physical dominance. For depressed students, words provide an avenue to relief. Student poetry, children's stories, and classroom discussion groups all provide opportunities to explore the richness of language in relation to human experience. Verbalizing feelings is interactive.

Teachers who model verbalizing feelings create a classroom climate that values communication. Many positive behavior supports, including "I" messages, accepting and acknowledging feelings, and Life Space Intervention help sustain the message that there are no such things as good feelings or bad feelings. All feelings are authentic expressions of internal states of mind and emotions that need to be accepted as legitimate forms of human expression.

Too often, teachers place value judgments on students' feelings by praising so-called positive feelings—joyful, happy, cheerful—while making it clear to students that such darker feelings as anger, resentment, and disappointment will not be tolerated. If impulsive youngsters are to learn to talk about their feelings, rather than act out their feelings, they must be allowed the freedom to express *all* feelings. Even an articulate child will remain silent without a teacher who listens.

RESISTING TEMPTING OBJECTS

Peter was one of my favorite students. He flitted from cheerfulness to anger like a sunny day abruptly turns into a Cape Cod squall. His difficulties with impulsive behavior almost always involved taking objects that belonged to someone else.

Redl and Wineman (1951) used the term "gadgetorial seduction" to describe children who are unable to resist tempting objects. The term was a semantic fit for Peter's behavior. He was literally seduced by any object that looked fun to play with.

His biggest problem was hoarding. Whenever a classmate would bring a new toy to class for recess, Peter would eye the object eagerly. I knew that unless I gave him time to play with or handle the toy, it soon would disappear. I never thought of Peter as a thief, because he had no use for the purloined object, and I always knew where to find a missing item. He buried all the objects of his desire in the same spot next to a split-rail fence on the perimeter of the playground.

A couple of years ago, I was visiting a classroom of one of the teachers who participated in the Preventive Discipline Project. While we were chatting, the teacher glanced across the room at one of her students and remarked sharply, "Mary, what are you doing with that test?" Mary had picked up the test from on top of a filing cabinet. Mary looked up and replied indignantly, "I didn't do anything. It just sort of jumped into my hands. You shouldn't have left the test on the filing cabinet."

Mary's comment underscores the helplessness that some young people feel when confronted with objects that beg to be poked, grabbed, hoarded, examined, or pilfered. The impulse to pick up an object, even though the negative consequences seem evident, is just too strong for a child with weak impulse control.

Youngsters who have difficulty with resisting tempting objects need help in order to learn how to control their impulses. They need distracting objects kept out of sight and reach. They need to learn more about their behavior. They need to learn how to reflect on the consequences of their actions before they act. They need opportunities to discuss their feelings about their behavior with an adult who is sympathetic to their plight. There is no joy in impulsive behavior.

I once encountered a fourth-grade student sitting forlornly on a window sill, staring out the window of the laboratory school where I have my office.

"Does your teacher know you are out here?" I asked.

"She sent me out here," he replied. I asked him why his teacher had sent him out into the hallway.

"You wouldn't understand," he said. "I have something called ADD, and I can't stop myself from getting into trouble."

His sad eyes and hopeless words spoke volumes about the need to understand impulsivity as a disabling condition that requires our best teaching efforts to surmount. The following four units present examples of how to incorporate activities that teach impulse control into daily lessons.

SKILL 1: MANAGING SITUATIONAL LURE

PHASE I

Teach the Concept

Take your class on a walking tour of the school. If the line spreads out or you have stragglers, designate certain spots as stopping points (Mannix, 1993). Go to the cafeteria, assembly hall, art room, computer room, and any other areas of the building that students typically need to use.

Give each student a pencil and paper and tell them their job is to inspect the premises. Have students look around each area carefully. Ask them to jot down suggestions to help improve the use of the area so that all students get the most out of activities without distractions. When you return to the classroom, have students compile their lists of suggestions for each area and activity. Present the list to the principal.

Read *Two Bad Ants* by Chris Van Allsburg. Prompt students to imagine the feelings of the ants during the reading. Brainstorm how the ants felt at various times in the story. Examine how initial positive feelings (e.g., energetic, curious, excited, etc.) deteriorated to negative emotions (e.g., fear, pain, regret) as they lost control of their situation. Discuss the title. Were the ants really bad, foolish, or naive? Discuss ways that young people can be attracted to various situations that turn negative. Design posters and decorate a bulletin board. Ask older students to describe why they go to a mall. List their reasons. Discuss positive and negative features of "mall life." Ask students to brainstorm other situations that start out as attractive activities and that can lead to trouble or danger.

PHASE II

Subskill

To identify appropriate behaviors outside the classroom.

Sample Activities

Social Studies

Introduce students to the Bill of Rights in the U.S. Constitution. In cooperative-learning groups, have students write and design "bill of rights" posters for hallways, the cafeteria, assembly hall, and so on. For example, in the assembly hall:

- I have the right to listen to the performance without distractions.

- I have the right to applaud at the end of a performance.

Ask the principal if student work can be posted in the appropriate areas.

Language Arts Ask students to write a short essay based on the "What If" theme. Some examples are:

- What if there was no highway speed limit?

- What if people could cut down any tree they wanted?

- What if it was illegal to yell at baseball games?

Encourage students to develop their own "What If" themes.

Brainstorm Ask students to describe inappropriate student behavior they find annoying:

- in the hallway

- in the cafeteria

- during art or other special classes

- during recess

- on the school bus

Cooperative Learning Make a "pet peeve" list on the blackboard, then organize students in cooperative learning groups. Assign each group a "pet peeve" topic and have them generate ideas for changing disruptive behavior. Come together as a large group, select the best ideas, discuss them, and forward the ideas to other classes for their input. Submit the final set of ideas to the principal.

Literature Read the book *No David* by David Shannon. As a group, ask the students to make a list of the inappropriate behaviors David exhibited in the story. Why were they inappropriate? Ask the children to think about why David acted the way he did. How was David feeling? The children can write a response to this question in their reading/writing journals.

Subskill   **To learn to adjust behavior to match the situation.**

Sample Activities

History/Social Studies   Using a unit in your curriculum, discuss how individuals had to change their behavior to adapt and survive. Some examples:

- immigrants at Ellis Island

- first settlers in America

- African slaves

Highlight how behavior and cultures change for the purpose of survival.

Science   Ask students to imagine the changes they will have to make in order to fit into our society in the year 2030. Have students draw pictures or do collages of their imaginary future cities. Discuss changes in behavior that will be required.

Literature   Read *Easy Does It: The Tale of Excitable Sam* by Margaret Hopkins. Discuss the book with the students. Record the main character, the problem, and the solution. Now read *Big and Noisy Simon* by Joseph Wallace. Follow the same procedure for recording. Finally, compare the two books. What was the common problem? (Curbing impulses.) How did each character resolve their dilemmas? (Changing their behaviors.) Hang the story charts in the room to remind the students how to control impulses.

Cooperative Learning   The students will read the first chapter in the book *There's a Boy in the Girls' Bathroom* by Louis Sachar. Now begin a class discussion. Why don't the children in the story like Bradley? What does he do that turns them off? What are some things that Bradley could do to alter the way his peers feel about him? Record the class list. Finally, ask the class to make some predictions about what will happen in the story. As they read, the class should return and check their predictions, making changes as necessary.

Cooperative Learning

Explain that each group is placed in a 5-day wilderness survival experiment. They can bring only 10 items to sustain the entire group. Have each group plan what to bring and justify the need for each item. Again, highlight the need to change behavior in order to deal with different situations.

POSITIVE BEHAVIORAL SUPPORTS

Proximity

Keep students with situational lure problems within close range and talk with them often about how well they are behaving. Also, buddy up impulsive students with role models.

Reality Appraisal

Students who cannot stop running or grabbing or pushing may have to miss important events, such as field trips. Highlight safety issues and explain that missing a trip is a *logical consequence* for disruptive behavior outside the classroom.

Rehearsal/Coaching

Walk students through the procedures required outside the classroom. Discuss with them the problems they have. Solve problems together. Ask students to repeat expected behavior in each situation.

Behavior Contracts

Together, write a contract describing the student's commitment to appropriate behavior outside the classroom. Have the principal and family sign the contract.

SKILL 2: DEMONSTRATING PATIENCE

PHASE I

Teach the Concept

Use cooperative learning. Divide students into groups of four. Have each group brainstorm situations that require patience outside of school. Use an overhead transparency to compile all the lists. Ask for suggestions on how each example of lack of patience could be changed into demonstrating patience. Write suggestions down. Talk about your own difficulties with patience and underscore that patience is not an easy skill to develop. Finally, ask students to make a commitment to change one way at school in which each of them is impatient. Stress the positive behavioral alternative. Make a commitment yourself.

At the end of each day, the students and you report on progress. There is no judgment in terms of failure, simply a discussion about the need to continue to strive to be patient. Keep in mind that you only are teaching the concept; behavioral change comes more slowly.

PHASE II

Subskill

To wait.

Sample Activities

Language Arts

Slow down the creative stage of writing. Teach webbing or semantic mapping. This intuitive method of generating ideas helps students learn to consider a variety of writing ideas. Editing comes later.

Semantic maps are like individual brainstorming sessions. Begin with a blackboard exercise including the whole class. Then have students develop themes with individual semantic maps. Follow up with traditional sequential outlines.

Literature

Read *Moose Of Course* by Lynne Plourde. Ask the children some discussion questions. Why did the boy have trouble finding a moose? What would have helped him? (Patience.) Now ask the children to write a variation of the story in which the boy does as he is told and waits to find the moose. Finally, compare the variations with the actual book.

Cooperative Learning

Read the book *Learning to Slow Down and Pay Attention: A Book for Kids About ADD* by Kathleen Nadeau and Ellen Dixon. The book covers school, friends, home, and the individual. Each child should look at his or her results and write an essay on the role patience plays in his or her life. Some questions to consider include: When am I patient/impatient? What are the causes? What can I do to help myself relax during times of impatience? How will I benefit from becoming more patient?

Across the Curriculum

Designate two students each day to be "teacher assistants." During individual work periods, these students respond to students who have raised their hands for help. Students write down problems that they cannot resolve and hand them to the teacher.

Subskill

To take turns.

Sample Activities

Across the Curriculum

Have a "You First" day. A few chosen students will give up their right to do things first. Secretly pick the students from the class and explain the exercise to them in private. At the end of the day, see if other students can identify the ones who were chosen. Follow with classroom discussion (Mannix, 1993).

Literature

Ask students what it means to take turns. Why do we want others to take turns? What happens when we don't take turns? Now the children can read individual copies of *Take Turns Penguin* by Jeanne Willis and answer a response question in their journals. The question should provoke critical thinking about taking turns and its advantages.

Cooperative Learning

Introduce the book *Being in Control: Natural Techniques for Increasing Your Potential for Success in School* by Jason Alster. In cooperative groups, ask the children to create a fictional story about taking turns. The groups will eventually perform their completed stories for their classmates, taking roles as if in a play.

Recess	Organize games, such as kickball, that require standing in line.
Spelling	Have a spelling bee. Two teams take turns spelling.
Language Arts	Students develop an oral story using a tape recorder. Students take turns adding sentences to the story.
Free Time	Provide board games that require taking turns. Match patient with impatient students to take advantage of modeling.
Learning Centers	Set up math and science activities that require sharing materials. Match impatient students with students who are patient.

Subskill

To help others.

Sample Activities

Social Studies	Ask students to imagine coming to school hungry. How would lack of food affect them? Locate a current-event article about world hunger. Read it to the class and tell the students to brainstorm ways to alleviate hunger. Make a bulletin board or posters to display in school.
	Ask the class to bring in canned food to donate during the next holiday.
	Contact representatives of a local shelter, church, temple, or mosque. Ask how your class could help, and invite the representative to speak to your class.
	Discuss the need to continue to help with social problems, no matter how big they seem.
Mathematics	Set up a math cross-age tutoring program with children from another classroom. Find ways to involve all your students. During feedback sessions, discuss with your students ways to be a patient tutor.
Language Arts	An alternative to math is a reading tutorial program.
Literature	Launch a unit based on the theme of helping others during November or December (right around the

holidays). Allow children to see and hear a variety of stories about helping others such as *Uncle Willie and the Soup Kitchen* by Dyanne Disalvo-Ryan, *The Lady in the Box* by Ann McGovern, *Helping Mom* by Mercer Mayer, and *The Mitten Tree* by Candace Christiansen. Have the class brainstorm ways they can help others, and create a class-helping project to be carried out at the close of the unit.

Cooperative Learning

Share the book *Somewhere Today: A Book of Peace* by Shelly Moore Thomas. This is a poem about people helping others. Then ask the students to expand the poem. Each student should create his or her own page for the book. Put all of the completed pages together to form a class book on helping others. The students can take their book into the primary classrooms and share it with younger children to inspire the tradition of helping others.

POSITIVE BEHAVIORAL SUPPORTS

Modeling

After asking a student a question, wait at least 5 seconds for a response. When a student is disruptive, allow 10 seconds between your desist and your next comment. When there is a classroom problem, listen to the student's point of view before making a judgment.

"Withitness"

At any given time, several students may need help. Keep aware of who is getting restless, who has his or her hand up, and who can tolerate waiting more than another student can. Ask students to help each other.

Intermittent Reinforcement

Give stickers or other tangible reinforcers for "good waiting." If you try to reinforce every situation, you will be running around in circles. Occasional reinforcement keeps students alert and lets them know you appreciate their efforts.

Restructure

Impatient behavior will accelerate when students lose interest in a lesson. Keep lessons brief, and do not hesitate to shift gears into a different activity if students are restless.

SKILL 3: VERBALIZING FEELINGS

PHASE I

Teach the Concept

Ask students to close their eyes, to imagine the following situations, and to describe the feelings that each image evokes.

- A field trip to the zoo is canceled because of rain.

- A bully in the playground during recess starts pushing you around.

- You get a bonus recess for good work.

- You have to move and transfer to a different school.

- Your best friend asks you to go on a camping trip.

- While walking down the street, you find a $10 bill.

- The principal announces that summer vacation will start a week early this year.

After students respond to each statement, write student feelings on the blackboard. After the lists are complete, ask students to pick out a favorite and a least favorite feeling. Have all the students explain their choices. Distribute art materials and have each student draw a picture that displays a favorite and least favorite feeling. Ask students to talk about their pictures. Emphasize the importance of knowing how you feel.

PHASE II

Subskill

To build a feeling vocabulary.

Sample Activities

Language Arts

Select a children's story that deals with feelings, and read it aloud in class. Stop to discuss with students what is happening in the story.

- Primary books:

- *Little Wolf* by Ann McGovern. This is a story about how a young boy deals with ridicule.

- *Annie and the Old One* by Misha Miles. This story deals with learning to accept the death of a relative.

- *Letter to Amy* by Ezra Jack Keats. A boy invites a girl to his birthday party.

• Elementary books:

- *I Won't Go Without a Father* by Muriel Stanek. A young boy refuses to go to a school open house because he does not have a father.

- *My Dad Lives in a Downtown Hotel* by Peggy Mann. This is a story about family separation.

- *The Tenth Good Thing about Barney* by Judith Viorst. Children have a funeral for a cat and recall memories.

Webbing Write the word "feelings" in the middle of a piece of chart paper. Gather input from the class and map out a web of different feelings. Record different types of feelings as well as their causes and effects. Hang the chart in the classroom for a visual reference.

Subskill

To **identify one's own feelings.**

Sample Activities

Language Arts Have students keep journals in special notebooks. Provide time to write each day.

Literature To familiarize children with the concept of feelings, read the book *The Oceans of Emotions* by Nicole Clark. This story contains valuable lessons about emotions and feelings, including the influence of words and choices, and taking responsibility for how we feel, act, and who we are to become in life. After the reading, ask students to respond to the story in their journals. Then ask them to write about their own feelings.

Role-Playing A wizard comes to town carrying a sack of magical clothing: the belt of happiness, the cap of frustration, the coat of disappointment, the tie of sadness, the gloves of anger. To wear items for the day, students must tell stories about why they deserve each item. The first time, the teacher can role-play the wizard; later, students can play the wizard.

Across the Curriculum Encourage students to identify their feelings during various activities. For example, a math worksheet might be frustrating, a science lesson might be disappointing, or a story might be sad. Support students talking about their feelings throughout the day by asking, "How do you feel about. . . ?"

Subskill

To identify feelings in others.

Sample Activities

Social Studies Ask students to put themselves in the shoes of the people they are studying. Some examples:

- What feelings prompted the Boston Tea Party?

- How did Native Americans feel as the white settlers destroyed the wilderness?

- How did it feel to be a 10-year-old slave in 1820?

Bring in newspaper articles that tell moving stories about real-life people. Have students discuss how various individuals feel.

Language Arts Use metaphors to encourage empathy in writing. Direct students to describe how it feels to be:

- a washing machine

- an old pair of roller skates

- a neglected stuffed animal

- a cube of sugar

- a bag of candy

Younger students can tape-record stories.

Literature Read the book *Chrysanthemum* by Kevin Henkes. Discuss how Chrysanthemum was feeling throughout the story. How did she feel about her name in the beginning of the story, in the middle, and in the end? How did the other students affect how she was feeling? Do the same with the book *Wemberly Worried* also by Kevin Henkes.

Cooperative Learning

Assign *The Janitor's Boy* by Andrew Clements for students to read. Allow them to read the novel over a period of time. The students can then complete a project based on feelings. The students will identify how Jack was feeling at different points throughout the novel and organize their information in creative ways. Encourage students to share their projects with the group before they are collected.

Cooperative Learning

Provide each group with poster board, scissors, and magazines. They are going to make "feelings posters." See how many pictures students can locate that represent different feelings.

Charades

Write various feelings on index cards. Have students pantomime and identify the portrayed feelings.

Subskill

To share feelings.

Sample Activities

Literature

Read the book *Do Animals Have Feelings Too?* by David Rice. Now ask for volunteers to demonstrate for the class how different animals express their feelings in different ways. Then ask if all people express their feelings the same way. What are some examples of how humans express their feelings? Finally, give each child a piece of paper with a feeling written on it. The children should use art to express the feeling. The class can attempt to guess all of the feelings their peers created based on the artwork.

Cooperative Learning

Have the class brainstorm many different ways to share their feelings. Make a list on the board or on chart paper. Now ask the students to select three ways they most often share their feelings. These can be from the class list or their own ideas. Encourage the students to elaborate on their methods of sharing feelings. Do they think these methods are successful? Could they do anything differently to help themselves share their feelings? Ask the students to try alternate ways of sharing their feelings over the next week and discuss the results at the end of the time period.

Role-Playing
Choose a conflict situation to play out. First ask the audience how characters felt, then ask players how they felt. Some suggestions:

- Your best friend tells you that she hates you.

- You are grounded for a week.

- Your family pet dies unexpectedly.

- A classmate makes fun of you.

Note: These types of role plays can bring on intense emotions. Carefully select themes and players. Provide ample time for student feelings. Be especially aware of quiet students who may be experiencing strong feelings.

Language Arts
Read "Benjamin Bunn" from Shel Silverstein's *Where the Sidewalk Ends*. Ask students how it feels to be different or how it feels to be disabled. Ask students to discuss times when they felt different.

Classroom Discussions
Set aside time each day, preferably at the beginning or end of the day, for students to discuss their feelings.

Elementary: You could begin an end-of-the-day discussion by asking students how their day went.

Primary: Have an object, such as a stuffed animal or "feelings stone," that students pass to each other before talking.

POSITIVE BEHAVIORAL SUPPORTS

"I" Messages
Identify and talk about your feelings. This modeling provides a constant reminder that feelings are important.

When you are upset with a student, report your feelings without saying it is the student's fault. For example, "Allen, I get frustrated," rather than saying, "Allen, you are making me frustrated." By taking ownership of your feelings, you are helping young-sters avoid the habit of playing the victim.

Hypodermic Affection

Children need to hear caring messages. They do not leave their emotional baggage at the school door. A child's life outside of school can be emotionally draining. Let your students know that while academic work is important, their lives, their feelings, and their welfare are your primary concern.

Life Space Intervention

Students in crisis need to ventilate feelings before they can deal with the concrete realities of changing their behavior. Life Space Intervention provides students with the opportunity to drain off strong feelings before moving on to the difficult stage of dealing with consequences.

Accept and Acknowledge Feelings

Underscore the notion that all feelings are legitimate. You may not agree with a student's feelings or even like the feelings being expressed, but they are the student's reality. Denying feelings only creates resistance. Listening and accepting does not endorse feelings, but it does demonstrate that you respect and care about a child.

SKILL 4: RESISTING TEMPTING OBJECTS

PHASE I

Teach the Concept

Videotape three Saturday morning commercials from network television. Before showing each commercial, ask students to write down the methods used by advertisers to entice children to buy their products. Show the commercials and let children write as they view each. Have a class discussion regarding the children's critiques. Encourage students to think about the allure of objects and ask them to talk about why objects seen on television seem so enticing. Brainstorm with students reasons why children need to learn to resist tempting objects seen on television.

Introduce the word "materialism" during your brainstorming session. Have students do a bulletin board project or posters on how materialism is directed at children and what children and families can do to resist materialism.

PHASE II

Subskill

To discuss how the allure of material objects can influence behavior.

Sample Activities

Social Studies

Bring in newspaper and magazine articles describing youths committing crimes to obtain material goods. Read the articles aloud, and have students discuss their feelings about committing violence to take such items as jewelry, sports shoes, and athletic jackets.

Language Arts

Have each student write a short essay on youth crime, its causes and outcomes. An alternative activity is to have small groups of students tape-record stories.

Language Arts

Have each student write an essay about a particular alluring object. What qualities does the object have that make it so desirable? What would the student do in order to get this object?

Literature Read the book *Junie B. Jones Is Not a Crook* by Barbara Park to the class to illustrate the concept of tempting objects. What attracted Junie to the pen? Why do you think someone stole her black mittens? Challenge the students to think critically about why we are attracted to material objects.

Subskill To evaluate the need for material objects.

Sample Activities

Literature Read *Sarah, Plain and Tall* by Patricia MacLachlan aloud to the students. Have them name some of the material objects mentioned in the book and create a list. Now ask the children to circle the objects on the list that the characters really needed and cross off those that served other purposes. Tomie dePaola's *The Legend of Bluebonnet* is also a book that focuses on material objects.

Read *Esperanza Rising* by Pam Muñoz Ryan. As the students read the novel, they should be aware of the role that material objects play in the life of Esperanza. How does her need for material objects change throughout the novel?

Cooperative Learning Have each group describe a list of items they would need for survival in the woods.

Mathematics Use lists written cooperatively by groups as a basis for calculating the costs of survival equipment. Check estimates against prices in camping equipment catalogues.

Using newspaper advertisements, have students work in pairs to calculate best buys in:

- automobiles

- groceries

- apartments

- any other items that lend themselves to comparison shopping

Subskill To use objects appropriately.

Sample Activities

Literature
Have the class brainstorm a list of objects they would take with them if they went camping. Ask the children if they think they know how to use each object appropriately. Then read *Outdoor Survival Handbook for Kids* by Willy Whitefeather aloud to the class to see if they were correct.

Across the Curriculum
Have a classroom discussion about how to organize the classroom materials. Use shelves and storage bins with labels. Discuss sanctions for misusing materials. Post safety and courtesy rules near learning centers. Provide free time each day for students to play games, paint, draw, and experiment with materials.

POSITIVE BEHAVIORAL SUPPORTS

Logical Consequences
If students misuse an object, they lose the privilege of using it for a day. Connect the consequence to the infraction.

Proximity
Know your students. Who is most likely to misuse materials or take something that does not belong to them? Proximity helps support self-control.

"Withitness"
Let students know you are aware of what is happening around the room. Stop misuse before it begins.

Alerting
Give students time to wind down in activities that they are enjoying. Provide support for the transition to another activity.

REFERENCES

Alster, J. (2001). *Being in control: Natural techniques for increasing your potential for success in school*. Rainbow Cloud.

Christiansen, C. (1997). *The mitten tree*. Golden, CO: Fulcrum Kids.

Clark, N. (1999). *The oceans of emotions*. Cocoa Beach, FL: PremaNations Publishing.

Clements, A. (2000). *The janitor's boy*. New York: Simon & Schuster.

dePaola, T. (1983). *Legend of Bluebonnet*. New York: Putnam.

Disalvo-Ryan, D. (1991). *Uncle Willie and the soup kitchen*. New York: Morrow Junior.

Henkes, K. (1991). *Chrysanthemum*. New York: Greenwillow Books.

Henkes, K. (2000). *Wemberly worried*. New York: Greenwillow Books.

Hopkins, M. (1996). *Easy does it: The tale of excitable Sam*. New York: Scholastic.

Judson, S., ed. (1984). *A manual on nonviolence and children*. Philadelphia: New Society Publishers.

Keats, E. J. (1968). *Letter to Amy*. New York: Harper & Row.

MacLachlan, P. (1985). *Sarah, plain and tall*. New York: Harper & Row.

Mann, P. (1971). *My dad lives in a downtown hotel*. New York: Avalon Books.

Mannix, D. (1993). *Social skills activities for special children*. West Nyack, NY: The Center for Applied Research in Education.

Mayer, M. (2000). *Helping Mom*. New York: McGraw Hill.

McGovern, A. (1965). *Little wolf*. New York: Scholastic.

McGovern, A. (1997). *The lady in the box*. New York: Turtle Books.

Miles, M. (1971). *Annie and the old one*. New York: Little, Brown.

Nadeau, K., & Dixon, E. (1997). *Learning to slow down and pay attention: A book for kids about ADD*. Washington, DC: Magination.

Park, B. (1997). *Junie B. Jones is not a crook*. New York: Random House.

Paulsen, G. (1987). *Hatchet*. New York: Bradbury Press.

Plourde, L. (1999). *Moose of course*. Camden, ME: Down East Books.

Redl, F., & Wineman, D. (1951). *Children who hate*. New York: Free Press.

Rice, D. (1999). *Do animals have feelings too?* Nevada City, CA: Dawn Publications.

Ryan, P. M. (2000). *Esperanza rising*. New York: Scholastic.

Sachar, L. (1987). *There's a boy in the girls' bathroom*. New York: Knopf.

Shannon, D. (1998). *No David*. New York: Blue Sky Press.

Silverstein, S. (1974). *Where the sidewalk ends*. New York: Harper & Row.

Stanek, M. (1972). *I won't go without a father*. Chicago: Albert Whitman & Co.

Thomas, S. M. (1998). *Somewhere today: A book of peace*. Morton Grove, IL: Albert Whitman.

Viorst, J. (1988). *The tenth good thing about Barney*. New York: Aladdin Books.

Wallace, J. (2001). *Big and noisy Simon*. New York: Hyperion Press.

Whitefeather, W. (1990). *Outdoor Survival Handbook for Kids*. Tuscon: Harbinger House.

Willis, J. (2000). *Take turns Penguin!* Minneapolis: Carolrhoda Books.

Following School Routines

7

I n order to follow school routines, a student must follow rules, organize school materials, accept evaluative comments, and make classroom transitions. These self-control skills are the infrastructure of every primary and elementary classroom. They constitute what sociologist Phillip Jackson (1968) referred to as the "hidden curriculum" of public schools. The hidden curriculum refers to institutional codes of behavior that typify classrooms. Students who master the hidden curriculum succeed; those who have difficulties are at risk of school failure.

FOLLOWING RULES

Young people have to learn to adjust to norms for behavior in different settings. Elijah Anderson (1994) notes that the "code of the streets" demands building a tough image. In poor urban areas, ostentatious display of objects, such as sneakers, jewelry, and athletic team jackets, reflects taste and a willingness to defend one's possessions. Violence is perceived as a necessary survival skill in neighborhoods where one gains respect by putting someone else down, either verbally or physically.

In school, behaviors that earn respect on the streets can get a child into serious trouble. Having to adapt to the rules of different environments places many youngsters in a dilemma. Which audience should they please in school: their teachers or their peers? It is no wonder that some urban youth break school rules when they are subjected to such conflicting pressures for respect.

Other youngsters may have difficulty with classroom rules and routines because of emotional impairments that interfere with their ability to reflect on and monitor their behavior. Students who are raised in chaotic homes frequently bump heads with school authority figures. These students need opportunities to learn and practice school rules on a daily basis.

However, as I learned in my days of substitute teaching, many students who behave when the teacher is present in authoritarian classrooms make trouble when the teacher is absent. Simply because students follow school rules when the teacher is present does not mean they have developed an internal sense of self-control.

ORGANIZING SCHOOL MATERIALS

Organization requires systematic planning, thoughtfulness, and the ability to make adjustments in pursuit of a goal. Organization is a fundamental skill for success. Disorganized students forget or lose assignments; they come to class unprepared; and they need prodding about their responsibilities. Students with attention deficit hyperactivity disorder (ADHD) are unable to concentrate on a task in order to see it through to completion. Other students simply do not understand the value of organization. They perceive organization as something one is born with, like the ability to draw well; you either have it or you don't.

Disorganized students are a constant source of frustration to themselves and their teachers. Such students need to learn how to be organized. They need to learn about lists, daily calendars, priorities, and how to break big tasks into smaller tasks.

Adherents of cognitive behavior modification believe that disorganized students need to be taught self-instructional strategies. The goal of cognitive behavior modification is to train students to use verbal statements for self-correction, self-evaluation, and self-reinforcement. The following four steps summarize how to use cognitive behavior modification in the classroom:

1. Cognitive modeling. The adult performs a task while verbally describing the task.

2. Overt self-guidance. The student performs the same task, imitating the verbal instructions of the adult model.

3. Faded, overt self-guidance. The student softly repeats the instructions spoken by the model.

4. Covert self-instruction. The student performs the task while silently instructing himself.

Teaching students how to plan is the basis of teaching organizational skills. It is a worthwhile classroom activity from which all students can profit.

ACCEPTING EVALUATIVE COMMENTS

Positive and negative comments in the form of grades, teacher comments, and remarks by peers are common in school. Indeed, by the time students have reached fourth grade, they can be so indoctrinated to teacher feedback that they lose touch with their own learning.

During my first year of teaching at a special education school, the teachers decided that we might get students to take more responsibility for their learning by involving them in grading their own report cards. We substituted "no improvement," "improved," and "much improved" for letter grades and held a conference with each student.

Later, my colleagues and I discussed the results of our experiment in student self-evaluation. Almost all the students "graded" themselves too harshly. The most frequent comment was "no improvement," despite the fact that many had shown significant progress.

Learning from mistakes, accepting constructive criticism, and accepting compliments are marks of maturity and perseverance. Students need to be able to acknowledge feedback, reflect on it, and make necessary adjustments in their performance.

MAKING CLASSROOM TRANSITIONS

Classroom transitions are the source of many behavior problems. While some students can handle confusion and remain focused during transitions, others get lost. They ask other students what they are supposed to do, and soon they are adding to the confusion.

Two common transition mistakes made by teachers are abruptly changing directions and "slowdowns." C.M. Charles (1989) described abrupt transitions as "jerkiness . . . the failure to move smoothly from one activity to another." He gives these two illustrations.

> *Suppose high school students are working on an art project. Unexpectedly, the teacher says, "Put your supplies away and get ready for a visitor." Half the class does not hear and the other half starts to move around in confusion. Or suppose an elementary class has just begun a math lesson. The teacher calls on three students to go to the board. On their way up she suddenly asks, "How many of you brought your money for the field trip?"*

She then counts the raised hands, goes to her desk, and writes down the number. (p. 32)

"Slowdowns" refers to time wasted between activities. Spending too much time giving directions or admonishing students for minor classroom infractions are two ways in which teachers disrupt classroom transitions.

For example, one day, my class was invited to watch a movie with two other classes in the auditorium. My students were excited, as were the other students. The teacher who was running the projector said that the movie would not start until everyone was quiet. Each time we thought he was about to begin the movie, he would stop to lecture a student about his or her behavior. At each slowdown, the students became more anxious and frustrated. The teacher finally lost his temper and announced that the movie was canceled. My students were in turmoil the rest of the day. Yet the whole unfortunate situation could have been avoided if he had just started the movie!

There are several things teachers can do to prevent behavior problems during classroom transitions:

- Give students a 5-minute alert and, if necessary, a 2-minute and 1-minute alert that an activity change is about to take place.

- Have materials for the next activity ready.

- Ignore minor disruptions and get into the next activity.

- Do not over-dwell on directions.

- Ask students who typically have difficulty with transitions to tell you what they are supposed to do.

- Initiate changes with serene music or recorded nature sounds.

Smooth management of classroom transitions is the cornerstone of a preventive discipline program. This is good news for the teacher, because it is an element of classroom life that rests entirely in the teacher's hands. The following four units present examples of how to incorporate the self-control skills involved with following school routines into daily lessons.

SKILL 5: FOLLOWING RULES

PHASE I

Teach the Concept

During the first class session, ask students to name some classroom rules that will help everybody to get along and learn well. Give students the opportunity to *brainstorm*. Then, as a group, select several of the best rules; emphasize the positive side of rules. Next discuss the consequences for breaking rules, but be prepared for students to suggest consequences that are too severe. Post the rules and consequences on the bulletin board, and review them each week for needed changes.

Set up a scene where a student has broken a school rule. Have several students take turns playing the teacher who is trying to understand why the rule was broken. Discuss different adult reactions to infractions.

PHASE II

Subskill

To understand why rules are necessary.

Sample Activities

Recess

Ask students to name their favorite recess games. Then tell them they should play a favorite game at recess, but without rules. If they agree, have a class discussion after recess. If they do not agree, discuss why rules are necessary.

Language Arts

Assign a brief essay titled "A Day Without Rules." Have students discuss their essays in class.

Social Studies

On the blackboard, list some laws with which students are familiar. Some examples might be:

- speed limits on highways

- seatbelt requirements for cars

- helmets for children riding bicycles

Ask students to determine the reasons for these laws. Then ask each student to suggest a needed law and to provide a rationale.

Subskill   **To identify with rules.**

Sample Activities

Science   Illustrate several "laws of nature," for example:

- the law of gravity

- warm air rises

- water freezes at 32 degrees Fahrenheit

- light travels faster than sound

Provide students with art materials and organize cooperative groups to design posters depicting various laws of nature. Next, discuss "laws of human nature." Ask students to develop a set of laws for helping people to get along.

Bring in newspaper clippings about domestic and international strife. Have students try to apply their "laws of human nature" to social problems.

Students can follow this activity by writing a letter to the editor of the local newspaper.

Cooperative Learning   Use the book *Play by the Rules: Creative Practice in Direction-Following* by Greta Rasmussen. This book provides about 50 activities that allow children to practice identifying with rules and following directions. The teacher orally reads the activity and it is up to the students to carry it out according to the rules.

Cooperative Learning   Send a note home asking parents to help students locate pictures and stories about a peacemaker. Some possibilities include Pocahontas, Mother Teresa, Martin Luther King, Jr., Gandhi, Albert Schweitzer, and Mikhail Gorbachev. Students should bring these materials to class and combine them with research materials available in the school. Each group presents to the class a 10-minute skit about the peacemaker they chose.

Literature	Read the book *Sammy Soccer Ball: Following the Rules* by Matt Jacobson, Henk Dawson, and David Ochsner. In this shaped picture book, Sammy the soccer ball teaches young readers the importance of playing by the rules. After reading, hold a discussion with the children. What were the rules in the story? What are some rules that you know? Do you have rules at home? Ask the children to write in their journals about rules.

Subskill To monitor one's own behavior.

Sample Activities

Mathematics	Review the classroom's positive rules for behavior, for example, "help someone" or "say something nice to another kid." Have each student select one rule that can be observed. Each day, the student will count how many times she or he follows the rule.
	Have students make their own counting books using folded paper and a stapler. Ask the students to make colorful covers. Organize the books by days; at the end of the week, have students graph their results. Discuss the patterns that appear in the graphs.
Literature	The teacher prepares a collection of different colored shapes cut out of felt for each student. He or she tape-records oral directions for turning the shapes into pictures. Some simple pictures might be a sailboat, a wagon, or a train. Each activity is numbered on the tape and corresponding pictures are drawn on cards showing the resulting shape. These cards are put in a box so that students can use them for monitoring and self-correcting.
Cooperative Learning	The activity described above can be adapted for the intermediate grades by increasing the level of difficulty of the oral instructions and terms. Pictures could be a clown, a skier, a vase of flowers, or a car.

POSITIVE BEHAVIORAL SUPPORTS

Reality Appraisal

Remind students about the reasons for rules. Encourage other students to state the reasons for rules. Also, ask students to describe what they believe are the consequences of their actions. For example, if a student keeps shouting out answers, how does that affect other students? What is the effect on other students of one student's temper tantrum? Again, pull other students into the discussion, thus taking advantage of peer pressure.

Proximity

By moving throughout the room, you nonverbally encourage students to follow rules. "Withitness" has the same effect. Essentially, you are letting students know that you are aware of what is going on at all times.

Restructuring

Minor rule breaking, such as talking, goofing off, and excessive moving around, is often a sign of boredom. Do not hesitate to change a lesson or activity that seems to be escalating into a series of teacher desists. Sometimes lessons are just too long.

Time-out

Removing a student from the rest of the class is particularly effective for students who want to be with their peers. Keep in mind, however, that some students would rather be in time-out than with the class. Use time-out judiciously, and keep a log.

SKILL 6: ORGANIZING SCHOOL MATERIALS

PHASE I

Teach the Concept

Role-play the scene "The Disorganized Teacher." The teacher and students play themselves. The teacher introduces the scene with the question: What is wrong with this lesson?

The teacher begins the scene by standing at the blackboard, facing the class, and asking for attention. The teacher is disorganized and cannot find his or her glasses, the chalk, or even the papers the teacher says will be distributed. Finally the teacher gets things together and begins the lesson, but he or she soon goes off on a tangent about summer vacation.

After the teacher spends 10 minutes hamming it up, the students discuss the scene. They give suggestions for improving the teacher's organization.

Highlight the need for organization in work. Ask the students to describe ways in which organization can help them. Make a list, and post the students' suggestions.

Follow up with a bulletin board and weekly theme on "Being Organized." Include several jobs, such as lawyer, surgeon, basketball player, coach, teacher, and student, and discuss how organizational skills are important to each. Have students contribute suggestions.

PHASE II

Subskill

To follow instructions.

Sample Activities

Mathematics

Have students try to follow a recipe in the learning center. The recipe should require the students to use fractions and measuring.

Listening

Before a student can talk during a classroom discussion on any topic, the student must paraphrase what the previous speaker said.

Primary: Such games as red light/green light can help students learn to follow directions.

Elementary: Construct model airplanes and cars from kits.

Subskill

To plan a task.

Sample Activities

Mathematics

Highlight the steps needed to complete math problems, for example, long division.

In the math learning center, have students use a stopwatch to find how long it takes them to complete math tasks; graph the average times for each week.

Time Management

Have students interview their parents and ask how they plan a week. Compare responses in a class discussion.

Cooperative Learning

Students can make posters on time management, using various occupations for inspiration.

Subskill

To organize materials to complete a task.

Sample Activities

Social Studies

In cooperative groups, students use catalogues, encyclopedias, and other reference materials to plan a 2-week imaginary trip through a country they have been studying.

Across the Curriculum

Students make lists of tasks to be completed during the next school day and tape the lists to their desks.

Teach students how to use a monthly calendar to plan.

Language Arts

Assign a 1-page essay on "The Day I Lost. . . ." Encourage students to describe their feelings and the problems that result from losing something. Primary students can take turns telling their stories into a tape recorder.

Subskill

To complete homework.

Sample Activities

Across the Curriculum

Divide long-term projects into smaller parts. Develop deadlines. Require parents to sign each assignment when it is completed. Take a few minutes at the end of each day to review homework assignments and to give students a chance to ask questions. Have students identify a time and place where they will complete their homework.

Literature Read the story *Jingle Bells, Homework Smells* by Diane de Groat. Have the children discuss what happened in the story. What were the consequences for not completing homework? How could Gilbert have planned better to get his assignment done?

Cooperative Learning Use the book *How to Do Homework Without Throwing Up* by Trevor Romain. Teach children about valuable homework skills like creating a homework plan and getting help with homework. This book contains many jokes, cartoons, and witticisms.

POSITIVE BEHAVIOR SUPPORTS

Alerting Give students 10-, 5-, and 1-minute warnings about when time is up to complete an assignment.

"Withitness" Stay in touch with how all students are progressing in their work. Keep an eye on students who have difficulties with organization.

Accept and Acknowledge Feelings Let students know you understand that organization is a difficult skill to learn. Share some of your problems; help students to avoid becoming discouraged.

Other Ideas Look for opportunities to provide structure for students. Lists of assignments on the blackboard, asking students to repeat directions, emphasizing the prioritizing of tasks, and encouraging parents to reward good organization at home are good possibilities.

Refer to *How to Reach and Teach ADD/ADHD Children* by Sandra Rief (1993). Chapter 8, in particular, contains many practical ideas for developing organizational skills.

SKILL 7: ACCEPTING EVALUATIVE COMMENTS

PHASE I

Teach the Concept

Role-play an impromptu conversation between a teacher and a colleague. The teacher begins a lesson on any topic; and after a few minutes, a colleague comes to the classroom door to speak with the teacher. The colleague is smiling and cordial, and he or she says that the teacher is doing a remarkable job. After a few minutes of additional praise, the colleague leaves. The teacher turns to the class and resumes the lesson. A few minutes later, the maintenance person knocks on the door to complain about how messy the room is every evening and to remind the teacher to close all the windows. (Compliments and complaints should be tailored to fit the situation.)

After the role play, the teacher asks the class to discuss their perceptions about what happened. Encourage the students to share their experiences with compliments and criticism. Put the words *compliment* and *criticism* on the blackboard and have students contribute examples of each. Pass out small note pads to each student, and call them "Feedback Books." Have the students record critical and complimentary statements they receive during the school week. Have a follow-up discussion at the end of the week.

PHASE II

Subskill

To learn from mistakes.

Sample Activities

Across the Curriculum

Emphasize the value of "wrong answers." Encourage students to estimate, to use their imaginations, and to make calculated guesses. The purpose is to help students understand that mistakes often lead to improvements.

Social Studies/Science

Discuss famous mistakes and their impact. For example:

- Columbus discovers America and thinks he has found a route to India.

- Napoleon and Hitler attempt to invade Russia and are defeated by the bitter winter.

- Alexander Graham Bell invents the telephone while trying to develop a hearing aid.

Brainstorm ways in which mistakes help in learning. Develop a list of "good mistakes" and post it in an accessible spot, then encourage students to add to the list whenever possible.

Subskill

To distinguish criticism from teasing, sarcasm, and mean statements.

Sample Activities

Brainstorm

Have students list all the "killer statements" they hear. For example: "That's a stupid idea." "You're weird." "Only girls/boys do that." Have students discuss how these statements make them feel. Continue to brainstorm ways of constructively expressing criticism.

Set up a suggestion box in the classroom so that students can anonymously make suggestions for improving the classroom.

Literature

Read the story *The Berenstain Bears and Too Much Teasing* by Stan and Jan Berenstain. Talk about teasing and being mean. Then ask the children how they can use constructive criticism instead of teasing, sarcasm, and mean statements. Make a class book of constructive criticism.

Cooperative Learning

Divide the class into groups of three. Assign roles in each group: a bully, a victim, and a criticizer. Each group develops a skit and performs it for the class.

POSITIVE BEHAVIORAL SUPPORTS

Hypodermic Affection

Let students know that you regard them for who they are, rather than for how well they perform in class. Keep in mind that students who have academic or behavioral difficulties receive many negative messages.

Make phone calls to all your students' homes on a regular basis, describing something positive about each student.

Accept and Acknowledge Feelings

Students with classroom difficulties are often discouraged. Help students identify feelings of frustration or disappointment. Point out "small victories," and keep students focused on their attributes.

Relate to Students' Personal Lives

Connect the curriculum in a meaningful way to student interests and their daily lives. A match between curriculum and personal lives enhances the intrinsic meaning of school activities. Motivation and perseverance, two key elements for success, will improve when students see the connection between what they do in school and the world in which they live.

Praise

Effort is more important than grades or correct answers.

SKILL 8: MAKING CLASSROOM TRANSITIONS

PHASE I

Teach the Concept

The teacher begins a lesson and abruptly begins talking about last summer's vacation. After a few minutes, several students are asked to go to the board to do some math problems. While the students are waiting for the problems, the teacher starts doing the lunch count. The students in their seats are told to read the next chapter in their social studies book (or any other text) until the lunch count is finished. The students at the board are ignored. Then the teacher says to those standing at the blackboard that she wants them to list as many state capitals as they can think of in 3 minutes. (With younger children, ask them to list their favorite animals.) By this time, everyone should be confused.

Stop the activity and discuss what happened. Lead the discussion with such questions as "What went wrong with our lesson?" "How did you feel about the confusion?" "What is a better way to proceed with lessons?" "How can we ensure that the same thing doesn't happen again?"

Highlight the need for schedules, routines, and clearly understood directions in getting work done.

PHASE II

Subskill

To follow the steps in a routine.

Sample Activities

Brainstorm

Ask students to help develop the best schedule for the class day. Discuss the need for schedules.

Try out different class schedules for 2 weeks, and then have the class decide which works best.

Mathematics

Present computational problems and ask the students to list the steps needed for solution. Compare the lists. Discuss the need to follow a logical sequence in solving some problems.

Across the Curriculum   Pair each student with a partner. Each student lists the steps in making a peanut butter sandwich. The partners then exchange papers and follow the directions exactly as written. Discuss how important it is to have clear directions in order to complete tasks.

Subskill   **To move appropriately around the classroom.**

Sample Activities

Writing   Have students work in cooperative groups to list reasons why the following are needed:

- aisles in supermarkets
- sidewalks
- fences
- streetlights
- guardrails on highways
- traffic lights

Discuss the reasons offered by each group. Then have the students select one of the above items and write a story about "The Day It Disappeared." Have the students read their stories and underscore how each thing on the list helps keep people moving and out of each other's way.

Brainstorm   Discuss the best ways to move around the classroom. Make a chart of "Do's and Don'ts" for moving around the classroom.

POSITIVE BEHAVIORAL SUPPORTS

Positive Reinforcement   Use a whole-group incentive to reward the entire class for smooth transitions. Draw a circle on the blackboard and alert students that an activity is about to change. Tell the students that you will count to a certain number; and if everyone has made the necessary changes without fuss, put a check in the circle. Provide a class reward for five checks in the circle. If students are unable to make a smooth transition, say, "Perhaps we can do better next time" (adapted from Rief, 1993).

Planned Ignoring

Do not draw attention to minor distractions. Your comments could create an additional distraction and provide unintended positive reinforcement. If you feel you need to let a student know you are aware of his or her behavior, use *signal interference.*

Proximity

Move about the room during transitions. Stay near students who you know have difficulties with movement or distractions.

Behavior Contract

The behavior contract (see p. 46) helps keep a student aware of specific appropriate behavior. Have the student clearly describe how she or he should proceed during transitions. Use the contract as a reminder that the student has a duty to respect the right of other students to learn.

Restructure

If transitions seem difficult for several students, look at what you are doing and make some changes. Consider some of the following:

- Give students an opportunity to stretch between activities.

- Follow a low-interest activity with a high-interest activity.

- Rearrange student seating.

- Review how well your classroom is organized, and make necessary changes.

- Shorten assignments or lessons to avoid satiation.

- Provide study carrels for students who are easily distracted.

- Make certain that supplies are ready before an activity begins.

- Discuss the morning and afternoon schedules before beginning class.

REFERENCES

Anderson, E. (1994). The code of the streets: How the inner-city environment fosters a need for respect and self-image based on violence. *The Atlantic Monthly, 273*(5), 80–94.

Berenstain, S., & Berenstain, J. (1995). *The Berenstain Bears and too much teasing.* New York: Random House.

Charles, C. M. (1989). *Building classroom discipline: From models to practice.* New York: Longman.

de Groat, D. (2000). *Jingle bells, homework smells.* New York: Harper Collins.

Jackson, P. W. (1968). *Live in classrooms.* New York: Hold, Rinehart, & Winston.

Jacobson, M., Dawson, H., & Ochsner, D. (1999). *Sammy soccer ball: Following the rules.* Grand Rapids, MI: Zondervan Publishing.

Rief, S. (1993). *How to reach and teach ADD/ADHD children.* West Nyack, NY: Center for Applied.

Romain, T. (1997). *How to do homework without throwing up.* Minneapolis: Free Spirit.

Tasmussen, G. (1990). *Play by the rules: Creative practice in direction-following.* Eugene, OR: Tin Man Press.

Managing Group Situations 8

Many students enter school without the ability to manage group situations. These students need to learn how to maintain composure when others are agitated or acting out. They need to appraise peer pressure in order to make good personal choices. They need to learn how to participate in group activities, and they need to understand how their behavior affects others. Among any class of students, there will be some who possess these skills and others who do not.

The group dynamics of a classroom present multiple opportunities for students to learn group leadership skills. Teachers can use group-process teaching strategies to capitalize on the strengths of the skilled students in order to help less-skilled students learn how to manage group situations.

MAINTAINING COMPOSURE

Many substitute teachers are familiar with the phenomenon of group contagion. One student acts up, another follows suit, and soon several or more are infected with the need to wreak turmoil. When I was a substitute teacher, I got firsthand exposure to group contagion. One class of fifth-graders begged me to let them play records at the beginning of the day.

"We'll be good, we promise," said Elaine, their persuasive spokesperson.

In my naiveté (and wishful thinking), I agreed, and I spent the rest of the day trying to deal with one uprising after another.

Even experienced classroom teachers deal with students who have difficulty maintaining composure when other students become overstimulated. Such ordinary events as returning from recess or the teacher briefly leaving the room provide these students with the stimulus to act out.

Students with difficulty maintaining composure need to learn to ignore classroom distractions. Learning-center activities help easily distracted students stay focused. Students who are doing something that engages them kinesthetically and tactilely are less likely to become distracted than students who are listening to a lecture or writing on worksheets. When students are bored or lulled into complacency by repetitious work, they will search out distractions.

APPRAISING PEER PRESSURE

As students mature, peer pressure outdistances both school and home as a motivator of behavior. A cursory glance around any sixth-grade classroom reveals how students copy each other in clothes, haircuts, and mannerisms.

Violent and troubled students are susceptible to negative peer pressure. Consider the appeal of gangs to young people. Frederick Mathews, writing in the *Journal of Emotional and Behavioral Problems* (1992), said:

> *Young people, by nature, tend to gather in groups. Peers are important confidants, models, supporters, and comrades in the developmental transition to adulthood. Gangs/groups give opportunities to try out roles, get support, and obtain security and a sense of connectedness and belonging. This latter point is especially true for abused, abandoned, or neglected youth. Gangs/groups provide instant access to power, self-esteem, and personal efficacy.* (p. 27)

Peer pressure is a natural part of growing up. But it is critical that students can select an independent course of action when exposed to peer pressure that leads in the wrong direction. Invitations to sex, alcohol, drugs, and crime bombard students from all directions. The more independent from adults that students become, the more susceptible they are to peer pressure.

Discussing peer pressure and engaging in activities that promote thought about peer pressure will help prepare students for those times when they are outside the helpful reach of adult guidance. Lecturing students about the dangers of "following the crowd" does little to stimulate independent thinking. Good choices about how to handle peer pressure require reflection, understanding of consequences, and practice.

PARTICIPATING IN GROUP ACTIVITIES

When teachers and administrators make a commitment to use group participation to enhance student growth, the results are impressive. Such collaborative learning approaches as brainstorming and peer tutoring make use of students as resources, while simultaneously teaching social skills. Group simulations teach students to work together to solve interesting problems. Positive group participation requires the ability to listen, to consult with others, and to negotiate decisions.

For example, students can be assigned the task of planning a 1-week vacation through Europe. Together, they must plan an itinerary, budget their money, decide on places to visit, and exchange money. Such simulations give students the experience of solving problems within groups.

The Phi Delta Kappa Commission on Discipline (1982) studied schools with impressive discipline records in order to uncover characteristics that typified good discipline practices. One of the central characteristics of effective schools identified was an emphasis on shared decision-making between staff and students. Student appeal boards, student participation in writing discipline handbooks, and student-community projects helped students learn responsibility by working toward common goals with their teachers and peers.

Rather than working effectively in groups, children with troubling behaviors try to use groups to meet their own egocentric needs. Such students distort group interactions by clamoring for attention, dominating, or quitting. These behaviors turn other group members against the disruptive student, and it continues the cycle of rejection that the troubled student so desperately needs to break.

Effective group-process skills can be taught both directly and indirectly. Pairing students to work together for brief periods on high-interest projects is a good starting point for indirect instruction. After a few successful experiences, more students can be added, until a small group of four to five students is formed. Attention needs to be given to the group composition so that student strengths and weaknesses counterbalance each other.

Highlighting group-participation skills makes sense, because students spend most of their school day in groups. Group participation is a common experience in every classroom. It is the ideal laboratory for extending student self-control skills.

UNDERSTANDING HOW BEHAVIOR AFFECTS OTHERS

The student refrains "I didn't do it" and "It isn't my fault" are familiar to every teacher. Accepting responsibility for one's actions is a developmental curve that many troubled youngsters have failed to negotiate. Their ability to gauge the effect of their behavior on others is stunted by the lack of reflection on their actions.

Fritz Redl and David Wineman (1951) characterize the lack of insight into contributing to one's own troubles as "evaporation of self-contributed links in the causal chain."

In spite of the barrage of lies and alibi defenses our children had available, we think we may safely state that sometimes they were not lying. Unless reminded immediately afterwards, the recollection of what they had done a short time ago was actually totally obliterated in the deluge of the incident that followed. A child involved in an exciting free-for-all with sticks and stones, may really not know that it was he who threw the first one to begin with. (p. 129)

One way to begin to learn about one's effect on others is through good deeds. Inside the most troubled student is a young person who wants to help others. Creating a climate of helpfulness and caring in the classroom puts a positive spin on the effects of behavior. Educational and community programs that empower youth teach them that they can make a difference in the life of another human being. It is easier to accept accolades for one's behavior than to accept criticism. By building on the basic human need to contribute, you can help your students learn that they can affect others in a positive or negative fashion. Once they understand the choice, the rest is up to them.

The following four units present examples of how to incorporate the self-control skills involved with managing group situations into daily lessons.

SKILL 9: MAINTAINING COMPOSURE

PHASE I

Teach the Concept

Role-play the scene "The Substitute Teacher." Select a student to take the role of a substitute teacher. Have several students role-play the class. Describe roles on index cards, which only the players see. Two students will "act out," and the rest must try to maintain composure and do their work. The rest of the class observes and makes a list of the disruptive student behaviors they see. Afterward, discuss how hard it is to maintain composure when others are fooling around. Ask players to describe their feelings. Have students identify times both in and out of school when it is important to maintain composure.

Follow up with a bulletin board about jobs that require the ability to screen out distractions; examples include surgeons, assembly-line workers, dentists, and firefighters. Discuss what could go wrong if these workers allowed themselves to become distracted or panicked. Look for newspaper stories that dramatize individuals who maintain composure.

PHASE II

Subskill

To ignore classroom distractions.

Sample Activities

Brainstorming

Students identify classroom noises they find distracting. Students categorize noises as preventable and non-preventable. Students and teachers discuss ways of coping with noises in each category.

Learning Centers

Ask students for ideas for learning centers. Make a list of materials that students can contribute. Getting students involved in setting up a learning center will enhance their ownership and participation in learning-center activities.

Peer Tutoring

Match students who have good attending skills with students who are prone to distractions. Give them tasks to complete together. This approach is useful for any curriculum topic.

Subskill

To independently select a classroom activity.

Sample Activities

Learning Centers

Establish a way for students to rotate between learning centers. One possibility is having 10-minute timers available at each center so students can monitor themselves. Manipulatives will help students to focus their attention and ignore distractions.

Literature

Provide a selection of reading material for the class and a list of response activities. Each student chooses something to read and a corresponding activity. Students work independently.

Subskill

To behave appropriately when the teacher is out of the room.

Sample Activities

Classroom Discussion

Use the following questions as a guide:

1. What would happen if the teacher left the classroom for a few minutes?

2. What do you think students should do when the teacher leaves the room?

3. Why do you think it is important for things to remain calm while the teacher is out of the room? (adapted from Mannix, 1993)

Language Arts

Elementary: *The Pinballs* by Betsy Byars. Children raised in a foster home learn to take control of their own lives.

Primary: *All the Secrets of the World* by Jane Yolen. Children have to learn to adjust to their father going to war.

In both of these stories, the scenarios require children to take care of themselves. Discuss how students have to learn to be personally responsible for their own behavior, even without adult supervision.

Look for heroes in children's books. Discuss why a person is identified as a hero. Highlight the point that heroes are independent thinkers who behave in a way they think is right, regardless of what others think. Have students list heroic qualities they would like to develop.

POSITIVE BEHAVIORAL SUPPORTS

Planned Ignoring

Each time the teacher reprimands a student, the entire class is distracted. One of the best ways to help students learn to ignore minor distractions is for the teacher to model the same behavior.

Proximity

By circulating around the room, the teacher helps students maintain composure without causing a distraction.

"Withitness"

Keep alert for behaviors that could cause a distraction, and redirect students.

Tangible Reinforcers

This approach is particularly useful for young children. Provide stickers or other incentives for ignoring distractions and completing work.

Restructuring

A leading cause of student distractions is lack of interest in a particular lesson. Watch for signs of boredom, such as staring out the window, shifting in their seat, or off-track comments. Shift into an engaging activity, such as learning centers or peer tutoring.

Life Space Intervention

Conduct Life Space Intervention with students who consistently lose composure when the teacher is not in the room. Try to identify causes for student behavior and help the students develop a plan for changing behavior.

SKILL 10: APPRAISING PEER PRESSURE

PHASE I

Teach the Concept

Ask students to tell you what they think the term "peer pressure" means. Once you have settled on a suitable definition, ask students to team in pairs. Each pair will list five examples of positive peer pressure and five examples of negative peer pressure. Discuss the lists in class. Put up a poster with the best examples.

Ask students to keep a record of examples of peer pressure they experience in a week. Each day, ask students to describe their experiences. Ask an adult who has had negative or positive experiences with gangs, clubs, teams, or other peer groups to come to class to discuss the pros and cons of peer pressure. Other possible speakers are police officers, community leaders, and clergy. This mentoring adds reality to your classroom discussions.

PHASE II

Subskill

To evaluate a situation in terms of personal beliefs about good and bad choices.

Sample Activities

Language Arts

Read the story "The Camel Dances" from *Fables* by Arnold Lobel. Discuss the moral of the story, "Satisfaction will come to those who please themselves." Encourage students to elaborate on things they do just because it pleases them, regardless of what others think.

Mathematics

Show students a large bowl filled with marbles or other small objects. Ask students to work in pairs to come up with some ways of determining the number of marbles in the bowl without touching the marbles. After the activity, tell students that social situations are often "sized up" or estimated before reaching a decision.

Ask students to estimate the consequences for the following scenarios:

- Your best friend tells you not to play with the new kid in the neighborhood because he or she is black, white, Jewish, or has a disability.

- You are captain of a team choosing sides, and you want to choose a kid who is always picked last; but you are afraid of what the other kids will say.

- Your best friend steals some money and wants to hide it at your house.

Writing   Ask students to write and illustrate a story describing how a kid could be stuck with a difficult decision because of peer pressure.

Subskill

To act in accordance with personal beliefs.

Sample Activities

Social Studies   Do a unit on one or more of the following Americans: Rosa Parks, Martin Luther King, Jr., Jackie Robinson, Nathan Hale, Patrick Henry, or other individuals who risked their lives for their beliefs. Use children's literature, guest speakers, videos, and art projects, such as drawing maps and timelines, to enliven the unit.

Language Arts   Ask students to define the word "hero." Have students make a hero list, but emphasize that the list cannot include people simply because they are celebrities.

See if students can identify everyday people who are heroes. Bring in newspaper and magazine accounts of heroic achievements. Have students write an essay or do a research project, titled "My Hero." Discuss qualities that students admire in heroes.

Cooperative Learning   Assign each group a "hero." Their task is to research the individual's life and do a collage, skit, or presentation about their hero.

Subskill

To identify peer situations where students should say "no."

Sample Activities

Brainstorming

Ask students to list peer situations that could pressure students into making bad choices. Write the situations on the blackboard and discuss alternative ways of dealing with each.

Social Studies

Select critical decisions in U.S. history and discuss what the consequences would have been if different decisions had been made. Some examples are:

- Lincoln decides not to sign the Emancipation Proclamation in order to end the Civil War.

- Harry S. Truman decides to invade Japan, rather than drop the atomic bomb.

- George Washington declines the Continental Congress's invitation to lead the revolutionary forces and decides to join forces with those loyal to King George in order to protect his home, farm, and investments.

- Rosa Parks gives up her seat in the front of the bus to a white woman.

- Rather than risk war with the Soviet Union, John F. Kennedy decides to allow the Russians to maintain their missile bases in Cuba.

Underscore that in each of these situations, the individual was under enormous pressure from various groups.

POSITIVE BEHAVIORAL SUPPORTS

Accept and Acknowledge Feelings

Peer pressure strongly motivates behavior, even for adults, as we all have a need to be accepted. By pointing this out to students, you can let them know you understand why they chose to follow along with peers. Encourage students to keep trying and recognize that everyone succumbs to peer pressure at some point.

Behavioral Contract

Help students identify situations that typically cause them to follow the crowd. Ask the student to make a commitment to pick the best alternative to such situations and identify the behavior that he or she will follow.

Sane Messages

Students need practice in understanding that there are always options when dealing with peer pressure. Sane messages spell those options out in concrete language without attacking the students' character.

Life Space Intervention

Bad choices based on peer pressure often lead to unpleasant consequences. This is an opportune time to explore with a student the factors that contributed to a peer-pressure decision, and to help the student develop a plan for better alternatives in the future.

SKILL 11: PARTICIPATING IN GROUP ACTIVITIES

PHASE I

Teach the Concept

Organize students into small groups of three each. Give each group five boxes of plastic straws and a box of common pins (younger students can use alternative construction toys such as building blocks, Lego, or Constructo-Straws). Direct each group to work together to build a structure of their own design. Give students 20 minutes to work together. After the activity, ask each student to list his or her own contributions to the task. Share with other group members and determine agreement and disagreement about each student's contribution. Discuss group behaviors that help and behaviors that hinder group work. Have each student make a commitment to work on one helping behavior during the next group activity. Follow up the next day with a review and a group project in any selected curriculum area. Keep students focused on behaviors that help groups succeed.

PHASE II

Subskill

To help others.

Sample Activities

Mathematics

Begin a math peer or cross-age tutoring program. Begin with once-a-week tutoring sessions. Provide tips on how to tutor. After each tutoring sesssion, solicit feedback from students, and make adjustments.

Social Studies

Do a community survey of social programs. Make a class trip to a homeless shelter, soup kitchen, or nursing home. Or invite representatives of social programs to class. Select a social program that the class will support. Do bulletin boards, a fund drive, a car wash, and other activities to highlight community service.

Language Arts

Read "Helping" in *Where the Sidewalk Ends* by Shel Silverstein. Ask students to brainstorm behaviors that help others and behaviors that don't help others.

Have each student make a commitment to one helping behavior for a week. Each day review progress with students.

Subskill   To cooperate.

Sample Activities

Social Studies   Review the instructor's manual of a social studies text to determine sections that describe cooperative efforts. Arrange four students in cooperative-learning groups. Group members help each other identify as many examples of cooperation as they can locate in 15 minutes. Some examples:

- building the pyramids

- fighting battles

- passing laws

- building a dam

Follow up with students interviewing parents about ways they have to cooperate at work.

Mathematics/Science   Set up activities that require two students to work together.

Learning Centers   Make pairings with compatible students who don't normally spend time together.

Language Arts   Have students do a group story. Pass a tape recorder around the room; each student adds a section to the story. Play the tape.

Recess   Organize cooperative games.

Subskill   To contribute to group discussions.

Sample Activities

Cooperative Learning   Use for any curriculum area. Highlight helping roles with a large-group presentation; emphasize that there are many leadership roles in a group. Some examples are:

- "engineer"—keeps the group on track

- "detective"—asks questions to help move the group along

- "lawyer"—summarizes key points

- "coach"—encourages participation; provides positive feedback

Brainstorm with the class and add others. Write down roles on an index card and distribute one to each group member. Secretly, each member attempts to act out a role during a group activity. At the end of the activity, members try to guess each person's role. Continue to highlight helping roles during all cooperative group activities.

Cooperative Learning Present a problem or question to each group of students that will stimulate their thinking. The solutions should not be limited. For example, how could we earn enough money to go on a class trip? Or how can we make the streets safer when we walk or ride bikes to school?

Language Arts Have each student make a telephone out of two paper cups and a piece of string. Then group the children and present them with a topic to talk about. The children will talk to each other through their telephones.

POSITIVE BEHAVIORAL SUPPORTS

Proximity Move from group to group and monitor progress. Have individual conferences with students who are having difficulty. Interrupt group activity if necessary to discuss how the group is functioning together.

"Withitness" Monitor group dynamics in terms of helping roles. Be careful not to assume a group is succeeding because there are no obvious problems. Talk with group members individually about group dynamics.

Restructuring Change group composition regularly to avoid cliques from subverting group cohesion and to help students learn to get along and work with all class members.

Alerting Give groups notice of approaching time limits.

Planned Ignoring   Avoid jumping in to solve all group problems. Give groups leeway to work out their own solutions.

Sane Messages   Tell individual students directly why a specific behavior hinders the group, describe the behavior, and explain the behavior you want to see.

SKILL 12: UNDERSTANDING HOW BEHAVIOR AFFECTS OTHERS

PHASE I

Teach the Concept

For primary students, read *Who Wants an Old Teddy Bear?* by Ginnie Hoffman. Ask students the following questions: How did the teddy bear feel when Andy kicked him? Why did Andy run away from the teddy bears in his dream? Why did the teddy bears treat Andy badly? What did Andy learn from his dream?

For elementary students, read "Deaf Donald" from Shel Silverstein's *A Light in the Attic*. Ask the students the following questions: Why did Sue leave Donald? Do you think, later on, Sue was sorry she left Donald? Do you ever do things to your friends that you are sorry for later?

PHASE II

Subskill

To identify behaviors that affect others.

Sample Activities

Brainstorming

Ask students to list things that their friends have done that have made them feel good and things their friends have done that have made them feel bad.

Have each student sign a "Feel Good" contract in which they identify one behavior they will pursue to make others feel good and one behavior they will avoid that makes others feel bad. Put designs in the contracts that students can color, and display the contracts around the room. In a class meeting at the beginning or end of each day, encourage students to share their progress for a week.

Literature

Read the book *Olivia* by Ian Falconer. Then ask the students to write down everything that they can remember that Olivia did to affect others. Finally, talk about the results. Were her behaviors positive or negative, successful or unsuccessful?

Cooperative Learning   Tell the students that they are going to create newspaper articles. Instruct them to take a small notebook wherever they go for a whole school day and take notes on how students' behaviors affect others around them. The next day, have the class share their findings. Then direct the students to write a newspaper article about the affects of behaviors. One of the articles can be published in the school newspaper.

Subskill   To demonstrate helping behaviors.

Sample Activities

Mathematics   One day a week, let students move freely around the room to help other students with math problems. A student who needs help raises his or her hand, and the student sitting closest helps. Problems that two students cannot solve are put on the blackboard for the entire class to contribute helping suggestions.

Social Studies   Read *Brother Eagle, Sister Sky: A Message from Chief Seattle* by Susan Jeffers. Discuss the importance of caring for our environment.

With students, identify an area of the community or around the school that needs cleaning or beautifying. Borrow cleanup tools from parents, and ask a local nursery to donate some plants or seeds. Students can brainstorm how to organize the cleanup.

Ask a representative from a local nursing home to come to class to describe the needs of the elderly. Plan a visit to the nursing home around a holiday, and get students to plan how they can contribute to the quality of life of the nursing home residents.

Subskill   To behave responsibly.

Sample Activities

Homework   With the permission of parents, set up a homework hotline. Explain to parents that this is a way for students to learn to be responsible. Each day, schedule two students as the telephone "hotline." Students who need help call these classmates during a designated time, for example, from 7:00 p.m. to 8:00 p.m. Any problems that cannot be solved through the hotline are recorded by the students and discussed in class the next day.

Science

Place several plants in the classroom. Review with the students the proper care for each, and write care guidelines below each plant. Establish a schedule so that each student can care for the plants.

Have a few small animals in the classroom. (Hamsters are a good choice.) Set up a schedule for students to take turns cleaning the cages and feeding the animals.

Across the Curriculum

Think of typical maintenance jobs that need to be done, for example, attendance, lunch count, passing out materials, and allocating hall passes. Designate students to take turns handling these details. Note: Do not use these responsibilities as punishments or rewards. These responsibilities should be assigned independently of behavior problems.

POSITIVE BEHAVIORAL SUPPORTS

Negotiate

Rather than telling students what they did wrong, ask them to review their behavior. When you sense that a student is about to shift the blame to another student, ask the student to begin his or her next sentence with the word "I." Encourage students to solve problems, and support the students' ideas.

Time-out

Allow students to cool off and reflect on their behavior in a part of the room set up for this purpose. After no more than 10 minutes, ask the student to return to the group and describe what he or she was thinking.

Life Space Intervention

This intervention is ideal for helping students to recount their behavior and begin to accept responsibility for their actions.

REFERENCES

Byars, B. (1977). *The pinballs*. New York: Harper Trophy.

Falconer, I. (2000). *Olivia*. New York: Atheneum.

Hoffman, G. (1978). *Who wants an old teddy bear?* New York: Random House Picture Books.

Jeffers, S. (1991). *Brother Eagle, Sister Sky: A message from Chief Seattle*. New York: Dial Books.

Lobel, A. (1980). *Fables*. New York: Harper & Row.

Mannix, D. (1993). *Social skills activities for special children*. West Nyack, NY: The Center for Applied Research in Education.

Mathews, F. (1992). Re-framing gang violence: A pro-youth strategy. *Journal of Emotional and Behavioral Problems, 1*(3), 24–28.

Phi Delta Kappa Commission on Discipline (1982). *Handbook for developing schools with good discipline*. Bloomington, IN: Phi Delta Kappa.

Redl, F., & Wineman, D. (1951). *Children who hate*. New York: Free Press.

Silverstein, S. (1974). *Where the sidewalk ends*. New York: Harper & Row.

Silverstein, S. (1981). *A light in the attic*. New York: HarperCollins.

Yolen, J. (1991). *All the secrets of the world*. Boston: Little, Brown & Co.

Managing Stress 9

Daniel is a 10-year-old powder keg with a short fuse. His special education teacher is constantly on edge, waiting for him to blow. She never knows what will set him off. His hostility is triggered by events that seem trivial to others. Praise, criticism, or a request to work can produce a sudden rage. A remark to "settle down" can increase his anger until he is so out of control that he has to be removed to time-out. Invariably, his last remark as he is led out of his classroom is, "Why don't you pick on the other kids, why only me?"

Many students like Daniel come to school without the emotional tools needed to manage their stress. In 1999, 463,262 students age 6 to 21 were placed in special education services due an emotional or behavioral disorder (U.S. Department of Education, 2000). Most experts in the field of childhood mental health believe that for every student who receives help for behavioral or emotional problems, there are two troubled students who are overlooked.

Stretched to the limit by the stressors of difficult lives outside of schools, troubled students are stripped of the emotional resources needed to cope with the additional stress of schooling. Chief among their difficulties is an inability to adapt to new situations, cope with competition, or tolerate frustration. A change in routine, a failure to keep up with other students, or difficulty with classroom work is all it takes to set off a troubled youngster. Bereft of ideas for dealing with their stress, troubled students are further handicapped by their inability to alleviate their stress through appropriate activities, such as reading, talking, playing, or exercising.

Students need to learn how to manage their stress. The payoff, in terms of a smoother-functioning, more harmonious classroom, will more than compensate for the amount of time you will have spent incorporating stress management into your Self-Control Curriculum.

ADAPTING TO NEW SITUATIONS

Troubled students frequently are required to adapt to new situations. Foster home placements are one example. The revolving door of finding a suitable foster placement would strain the emotional resources of the most stable child, much less one who is growing up without the benefit of a nurturing adult relationship. Some children live transient lives—moving from one welfare hotel to the next—and they are the fortunate ones. Others wander the streets of urban areas, living off the largess of shelters, or worse, falling prey to abusers and drugs.

In school, many troubled youngsters are expected to adapt to new situations. Some are pulled out of their classrooms for resource room help, others meet regularly with counselors. Many are placed in self-contained special education classrooms. Adolescents frequently are placed in alternative high school programs; and, in cases where families are unable to provide for the child, students are placed in residential facilities. Each of these treatment programs means change and adjustment to new situations. Students who are unable to cope with the stress brought on by change will typically react with pretenses of familiarity, hostility, or ridicule. Redl and Wineman (1951) characterized these reactions as "newness panic."

Lessons about how others have successfully handled new situations lay a cognitive foundation for students to adjust to change. History is replete with examples of people starting over in new and challenging situations. Indeed, social studies could rightly be called the study of human adaptation. The survival of every culture is based on its ability to cope with changing conditions. Once models for adapting to new situations are familiar to your students, they will be ready to apply learned lessons to their own lives.

Encouraging students to express their feelings about their lives provides an outlet for their stress, while simultaneously modeling appropriate coping behaviors. Journals, short stories, class discussions, brainstorming, children's literature, and art work can be used by students to describe their feelings about change.

COPING WITH COMPETITION

Schools are immersed in competition. Report cards, tests, rewards, and positive strokes from teachers are all based on student performance. Invariably, each of these evaluation indicators leads to comparisons between students. Ability groups, tracking, and remedial pull-out programs are highly visible reminders that some students are less capable than others. For students who have a well-balanced emotional life, coping with competition is difficult; for troubled students, even mild doses of competition can prove overwhelming.

Both the pitfalls and the blessings of competition are well known to anybody who has won or lost at school, at work, or at play. Competition can raise one's spirit, and it can dash one's spirit. The ability to handle competition in an even-handed manner is a challenge for all of us. For troubled students, the task is more difficult. Competition generates instantaneous doses of stress that overwhelm their meager self-control abilities.

Classrooms that emphasize cooperation are less stressful and better suited to the needs of troubled students. In these settings, students learn to work with each other, rather than against each other. Rewards are intrinsically based on the pleasure the group derives from attaining its goals.

Working and sharing with others provides a bulwark against the inevitable setbacks of competition. Resilience in the face of competition is forged by a strong sense of self-worth. Activities that highlight student talents, provide natural, positive consequences, and encourage taking risks work best.

Competition is an unavoidable feature of life. You cannot protect your students from competition. But you can provide them with the tools they need to cope with competition both in and out of school.

TOLERATING FRUSTRATION

The ability to persevere in the face of frustration is a trademark of success. While teachers never purposefully try to frustrate their students, many every-day classroom affairs require the ability to manage frustration. Waiting for the teacher to answer a question, puzzling over a difficult math problem, and stumbling through a reading passage are common, everyday experiences for many students. To a large extent, how they handle these minor frustrations can make the difference between school success or failure.

Consider the following comparison:

- Alan is tired of waving his hand for help, so he starts doodling on a pad. As the teacher approaches, he slides the pad under his book.

- Alice has been waving her hand, too. Soon the waving is accompanied by "Ms. Durea, I need help." Ms. Durea, who is working with another student, tells Alice to be patient. Alice throws her workbook on the floor and puts her head down on her desk.

Both students were frustrated; but while Alan sublimated his frustration by doodling, a nonintrusive coping strategy, Alice caused a disturbance. Ms. Durea, in turn, may feel frustrated by Alice's reaction. The situation could easily take a turn for the worse if Ms. Durea overreacts. Alice will need some gentle coaxing to return to her assignment; and, unfortunately, this will take time away from some other student who also needs the teacher's attention.

One student's frustration can create a ripple effect in the classroom. Troubled students rarely suffer frustration in silence. They either act out their frustration or withdraw. Either way, they quit trying to learn. Their resultant low motivation and accompanying behavior problems can strain the energy of the most resourceful teacher.

To learn how to cope with the stress that accompanies frustration, students need to understand what is happening to them. Many troubled students do not even have the word "frustration" in their vocabulary. Attaching a word to their feelings is a critical first step to helping youngsters manage frustration. Next, students need to learn that frustration is a normal physical reaction to stress and is best dealt with by identifying those stressors that trigger frustration.

Once you have developed in your students an understanding of how frustration affects them, you can help them develop coping strategies. Sharing ideas about what works for some students is a good beginning. But no two students are alike, and eventually each will need to plot his or her own course. This will require reflection and self-analysis. You can support these efforts by encouraging students to talk about their frustrations. Help them to persevere by adapting assignments to meet their needs. For example, give fewer math problems; do not overcorrect their writing—that is, spelling and grammar; give them more time to finish assignments; provide a peer tutor; and, most important, avoid situations, such as oral reading, that would embarrass or humiliate a student in front of his or her peers.

SELECTING TENSION-REDUCING ACTIVITIES

As long as we are breathing and perceiving the world around us, we encounter stress. This may be a hard fact to swallow, because our society places such an emphasis on being "cool." Television advertisements tell us, "Don't let them see you sweat." Macho movie stars face down danger without blinking.

At the same time, in the real world, teenage girls diet and purge themselves into living skeletons. Suicide takes more young lives each year, and a generation of abused children turn into child abusers. In our schools, we warn students about drugs and alcohol. We tell them to avoid premarital sex. Meanwhile, teenage pregnancies climb, and students are drinking and smoking younger than ever. Clearly, young people are receiving a lot of mixed messages about how to deal with stress, and their behavior reflects their confusion.

The adult campaign to help youngsters learn how to manage their stress misses one critical element—modeling. Students need real-life examples that will counteract the cardboard models for behavior that the sports world and the entertainment industry prop up before them.

Classroom life offers unlimited opportunities to model stress management. Encourage students to talk and write about their feelings. Discuss your own feelings and how you manage stress. Teach students to identify signs of stress, for example: sweating palms, shortened breath, and nervousness. Discuss ways of dealing with stress in the classroom.

Provide options for students to ventilate stress. One teacher has a punching bag in her room, another teacher set up a quiet reading corner with a rocking chair, a third has students get up and stretch when she senses the stress building. Animals, plants, and quiet music are stress reducers. A relaxing classroom provides the basis for teaching stress reduction.

The following four units present examples of how to incorporate the self-control skills associated with managing stress into daily lessons.

SKILL 13: ADAPTING TO NEW SITUATIONS

PHASE I

Teach the Concept

Do a unit on immigration. Help students develop a questionnaire for their families. Include such questions as: Who was the first in your family to come to the U.S.? Where did this family member settle? What were some of the difficulties with which that family member dealt? Ask students to bring photos or other memorabilia to class. Discuss the difference between immigration and slavery. Show the first segment of the television series "Roots," based on the book by Alex Haley. Underscore the differences between life in the United States and life in immigrants' homelands. Highlight the ability of newcomers to adapt to the new environment. Include references to Native Americans and their relationships with the white settlers. Construct a bulletin board with the theme "Adaptation," and post pictures and stories of how different ethnic groups have adapted. Finally, discuss how it continues to be important to adapt to new situations.

PHASE II

Subskill

To identify ways by which people adapt to their surroundings.

Sample Activities

Social Studies

Contrast the lifestyles of the Plains Indians and Eskimos. Highlight adaptation by contrasting lifestyle, food, clothing, and shelter.

Use your community as a laboratory. Discuss how the nature of your community—rural, suburban, or urban—shapes behavior and community priorities. Ask a local politician to come to class and speak about community issues.

Have students brainstorm ideas about what their community could be like 20 years from now. How could students improve the community? In what direction would students like to see their community move?

| **Language Arts** | For primary students, read *Time for School, Nathan!* by Lulu Delacre. Discuss how Nathan and Nicholas Alexander adapt to school. Encourage students to discuss changes in their lives. |

For elementary students, read *Sky Dogs* by Jane Yolen. Discuss how the horse changed life for the Plains Indians. Ask students to identify one event that changed their lives. Encourage students to write and illustrate a story about "changes."

Subskill To cope with change.

Sample Activities

Role-Playing Set up a scene with a substitute teacher. Designate five students to role-play the class. On index cards, give each student a specific role with a brief explanation. For example:

- "Substitute teacher": Take attendance, lunch count, and begin a reading lesson.

- "Helper": Assist the substitute teacher to get settled.

- "Clown": Keep acting up to get attention from friends.

- "Shy student": Be quiet and withdrawn.

- "Adapter": Follow substitute's directions. (Select two students for this role.)

After the role play, have students guess the roles. Discuss the feelings of each participant. Talk about ways to behave when a substitute teacher is called in.

Language Arts Write the phrase "Life is always changing" on the blackboard. Have students discuss what the phrase means. Give students art materials and tell them to draw a "life-line" that highlights changes in their lives, for example: a move, the birth of a sibling, the death of a relative, starting school, and so on. Share the life-lines with the class.

For primary students, read *Peter's Chair* by Ezra Jack Keats. Discuss why Peter did not want his crib painted.

Ask students to discuss how they would feel in Peter's place.

For elementary students, read *My Dad Lives in a Downtown Hotel* by Peggy Mann. Discuss how Joe reacts to the change in his family. Highlight how change that seems negative can have a positive side.

Subskill   To direct one's own behavior.

Sample Activities

Learning Centers   Establish a "center time" as part of the school day. Develop a procedure for moving from one center to another. For example, have two seats at each center, and when a seat is empty, a student can go to that center. This self-directing activity will help students learn to work independently.

Peer/Cross-Age Tutoring   Taking responsibility is a major feature of tutoring. In regular feedback sessions with tutors, review situations where things do not go as planned and give students opportunities to share feelings and ideas.

POSITIVE BEHAVIORAL SUPPORTS

Proximity   Learning centers and other such student-centered activities as cooperative-learning groups and peer tutoring do not require continual adult direction. This enables the teacher to move around the room and provide nonverbal support by proximity.

Restructuring   When an activity or schedule is changed purposefully, it provides students practice with making adjustments in their daily routine. Restructuring also provides the teacher with clues about difficulties specific youngsters have with change.

Planned Ignoring   Changes always bring some discomfort or confusion. Allow students some leeway for frustration or disappointment.

Alerting   Give students notice of changes in routine or schedule in advance; this gives you time to explain how they will adjust to the change or new situation.

SKILL 14: COPING WITH COMPETITION

PHASE I

Teach the Concept

Share newspaper and magazine articles about losing in sports. Do this activity at the beginning of a sporting season; tennis, golf, baseball, basketball, football, and hockey are good choices because they get a lot of media coverage. Show pictures of losing players. Ask students to describe how the losing players feel. Ask students to predict how the losing players will handle the loss. Follow the exploits of the identified players for a season. Have students write a letter and ask selected players how they handle losing and winning. Keep track of how the identified player continues to persevere.

You also might follow the exploits of a player you identified as a winner. The concept you are teaching is that no one wins all the time, but, regardless of the outcome, competitors persevere. You also can adopt losing teams. Write to the coaches or managers. Ask them to explain to your students why they keep trying despite setbacks.

PHASE II

Subskill

To identify positive attributes of competition.

Sample Activities

Language Arts

Read these stories aloud to your students: *The Value of Facing a Challenge* by Ann Donegan Johnson. This is the story of Terry Fox, the disabled Canadian marathon runner. Another selection is the first book of a trilogy, *A Lady, A Champion* by Russell W. Ramsey. This is the story of a champion swimmer who is the founder of a swim school for children with disabilities.

Values Clarification

Rent the movie *Brian's Song.* Discuss the meaning of competitive spirit and the role it played in the friendship between Brian Piccolo and Gale Sayers.

Mathematics Use statistics on baseball cards to highlight math skills appropriate to ability levels.

- *Addition and subtraction:* Calculate differences in production between years.

- *Reading tables:* Ask students to find specific information, for example: How many home runs did Barry Bonds hit in 2000?

- *Percentages:* Batting averages and ERAs of pitchers.

Discuss differences between player production from year to year.

Subskill **To participate in competitive games.**

Sample Activities

Mathematics Have an auction with play money. Give each student $500 and explain how an auction works. Auction off stickers, pencils, and other inexpensive items. As students bid, they will figure out how to outwit classmates and will learn more about the relative value of money.

Language Arts Ask students to name an object or activity they enjoy, such as their favorite toy or their hobby. Write each word or term on an index card without other students seeing. Shuffle the cards and play charades. Students must guess by raising their hand. The winner comes to the front of the room, draws a card, and performs another charade.

Keep a list of your new vocabulary words at the front of the room. Write stories for students to read, using the new vocabulary words. Also have the students write stories using the same words or terms.

Learning Centers Allow students to play board games during free time. Have a three-student panel to mediate disputes. Students who do not display good sportsmanship will lose opportunities to play.

Recess Organize competitive games in which all students can participate, for example kickball or volleyball. Watch for how children handle the competition.

Take students aside and discuss how they are doing. Also, raise issues of sportsmanship in class. Encourage all students to discuss their feelings.

Across the Curriculum   Avoid competition for academic performance. Remember the perils of praise. For every youngster who is a winner, there are many youngsters who will feel disappointed. Emphasize effort; achievement will come if students can learn to persevere.

POSITIVE BEHAVIORAL SUPPORTS

Planned Ignoring   Allow students opportunities to manage their own disputes.

Alerting   Give students notice about an approaching time limit to end a game. Try to time the conclusion so that all competitors have had opportunities to contribute to their team.

Restructuring   Do not allow a competitive event to get out of hand. Observe how participants are handling the stress. If necessary, stop the action to discuss what is happening at the moment.

Rehearsal/ Coaching   Role-play competitive problems. Have students who have difficulties with competition role-play the referee or a parent. Broaden students' perspectives about how poor sportsmanship looks and sounds to others. Videotape a recess game and discuss in class.

Logical Consequences   In hockey, a player who is a bad sport has to sit in a penalty box. Students who gloat, sulk, or whine should be kept out of the next game, because of the negative effect their behavior has on other students' fun.

SKILL 15: TOLERATING FRUSTRATION

PHASE I

Teach the Concept

Write the word "frustration" on the blackboard. Ask students to try to define the word. After their attempts, look up *frustration* in the dictionary and write the definition on the blackboard. Then ask students if they ever feel frustrated with school work. Write the heading "Things That Frustrate Us about School." Tell them this is a brainstorming session and it is okay to say how they really feel. Give a few examples yourself, such as, "I feel frustrated when a class is interrupted by a schoolwide announcement" or "I feel frustrated when I'm late for work and I get caught in a traffic jam." Encourage students to think carefully, and do not criticize any of their ideas. Write the list on the blackboard. You can narrow the discussion by asking students to brainstorm what makes them frustrated in specific subjects, such as math, science, or reading. Follow up by asking them to think for a few minutes about things in their lives that make them frustrated. Set a timer for 10 minutes and ask them to write down all the things that frustrate them. They are not to put their names on their "frustration lists," but they are to hand them in to you. (These lists will give you ideas for follow-up activities.)

PHASE II

Subskill

To identify feelings of frustration.

Sample Activities

Across the Curriculum

Tape a "frustration barometer" on the desk of each student, using a piece of paper with a colorful design. Select a subject, and tell students to make a check on the frustration barometer each time they feel frustrated. Students do not have to explain why they put a check on their barometers. At the end of the period, have students tally their frustration marks. Keep a record of these incidents of frustration. Over a period of a week or two, take a frustration barometer for each subject.

Mathematics Have students tally their total number of frustration incidents for the period of data collection. Have them make their personal frustration tables or graphs, first by days and then by subjects. Discuss the results. Try to identify and record reasons for student variations in frustration.

Art Bring in copies of *USA Today* to show students various ways of showing data with tables and graphs. Encourage students to be creative in their own table and graph design.

If individual student frustration barometers do not record enough incidents, have students develop group tables and graphs.

Subskill **To develop methods for coping with frustration.**

Sample Activities

Language Arts Read "Deaf Donald" from Shel Silverstein's *A Light in the Attic*. Ask students how Donald felt. Ask them if they ever felt frustrated by not being able to communicate their feelings. Ask students to brainstorm behaviors that get in the way of communication and behaviors that help communication. Ask students to write a story about a time when they felt misunderstood. Share stories and have students discuss how they might have improved the situation for themselves or others.

Across the Curriculum Place a suggestion box in class. Any time a student has an idea to improve the classroom, he or she can put the suggestion in the box. All contributions are anonymous.

Social Studies Search newspapers and magazines for individuals who have overcome disabilities or other problems on the path to success. Some examples:

- Jim Abbott—a baseball player with one hand.

- Stephen W. Hawking—the eminent authority on black holes in space who has a motor-neuron disease.

- Thomas Murray—a one-legged basketball player on Panama's Special Olympics team.

- Mugsy Bogues—the shortest player in the NBA.

- Helen Keller—an educator with multiple disabilities.

- Ruby Bridges—as a 6-year-old, she integrated a New Orleans elementary school. She is the subject in one of Norman Rockwell's most famous paintings.

- Jackie Robinson—who broke the color barrier in baseball.

Discuss with students how individuals cope with frustration. Have students interview family members about how they cope with frustration. Give reports in class.

Mathematics Use error analysis in grading student worksheets. Rather than marking all incorrect answers, look for the basic mistake that is causing the wrong calculations. Error analysis also is useful for reading and spelling. It is a well-researched approach for students with learning disabilities.

Peer/cross-age tutoring Give students who have difficulties with a specific subject the opportunity to tutor younger students in that subject. This will build their confidence and improve their skills.

Also, use peer tutoring in your class, allowing students to help each other.

POSITIVE BEHAVIORAL SUPPORTS

Hypodermic Affection Be alert to signs of frustration in your students. Gently encourage them to try their best. Tell them stories about your frustrations in school as a child. Tell them to take a break before they become overwhelmed.

Accept and Acknowledge Feelings	Let students know that it is okay to be frustrated; it is a natural feeling when one is trying to do well.
"Withitness"	At any given moment, at least one or two students are experiencing some frustration with their work. Become adept at identifying these students and attending to them right away.
Positive and Intermittent Reinforcement	Give students incentives to persevere. Emphasize that effort is most important when dealing with frustration.

SKILL 16: SELECTING TENSION-REDUCING ACTIVITIES

PHASE I

Teach the Concept

Conduct a class discussion about stress. Write the word "stress" on the blackboard and ask students what it means. Responses might include "stressed out" and other expressions with which students are familiar. Emphasize that stress causes tension. Demonstrate with a balloon: "See how the skin of the balloon stretches as more air (stress) is added." Ask students to predict what will happen if you keep blowing into the balloon.

Explain that stress causes tension, and, unless the tension is alleviated, the consequences can be harmful. Ask students if they ever feel tense, and write situations that cause stress on the board. Ask students what they do when they feel stress. Classify responses into harmful and healthful stress reactions. Discuss how such activities as exercise, reading, and playing help reduce stress.

PHASE II

Subskill

To identify physical signs of stress.

Sample Activities

Science

Have students take each other's pulse and record the number of heartbeats in a minute. Then have students do two minutes of calisthenics and measure each other's pulse again. Compare the results. Follow the same routine with a stethoscope.

Mathematics

Students keep a record of their resting and post-exertion pulse rates and calculate the average for a week.

Subskill

To identify situations that cause stress.

Sample Activities

Social Studies

Every major change in history is prompted by social stressors. Discuss the Vietnam War and how demonstrations put pressure on the government to withdraw the U.S. forces. Read about and discuss the American Revolution or Civil War and have students review events that created social pressure for change.

Language Arts

Begin by describing a stressful day when you were the same age as your students. Have students make a list of things that cause them stress. Write the list on the blackboard.

Organize students in pairs. Give each pair poster board and markers, and direct students to make a poster, titled "Stop this Stressor." They can select any item or combination from the board. Conclude this activity by telling each student to imagine they have been given a single wish that will make any stressor in their life disappear, but, in order to be awarded the wish, they have to write a brief essay, titled "Why I Deserve a Wish."

Subskill

To identify tension-reducing activities.

Sample Activities

Across the Curriculum

Play calming music in class during times when students might be susceptible to stress. During transitions, while doing independent seatwork, or near the end of the school day are some possibilities. Environmental audiotapes and compact discs are other options.

Students need to have stress-reducing activities available in the classroom. Some suggestions: a rocking chair, punching bag, arts and crafts table, quiet reading area, or computer. Students need options so they can practice selecting a tension-reducing activity that meets their needs.

Centerplay: Focusing Your Child's Energy by Holly Young Huth contains many stress-reducing activities, including deep breathing, yoga exercises, meditation, visualization, and relaxation techniques.

Literature

Prepare the room for listening enjoyment. Ask the students what environment helped them listen to stories when they were younger and allow them to describe their previous experiences. Have them list books and the feelings they associate with them. Now read aloud to the students or have students read to each other in an environment they find tension-reducing.

POSITIVE BEHAVIORAL SUPPORTS

Life Space Intervention

Review with the student the plan for dealing with a critical incident. Highlight options for avoiding stressful situations.

Modeling

Allow students to see you responding to stress. Take a few deep breaths; count to ten out loud; change an activity that you find frustrating.

Accept and Acknowledge Feelings

Ask students if they are feeling stress. Help students clarify their feelings. Help students resolve the stressful situation by offering options.

Time-out

Take a nonpunitive approach and tell the student to take some time to calm down in an area of the room designed for this purpose. It could be a rocking chair, a quiet place to read or just to sit and think.

REFERENCES

Delacre, L. (1989). *Time for school, Nathan!* New York: Scholastic.

Huth, H. Y. (1984). *Centerplay: Focusing your child's energy.* New York: Fireside.

Johnson, A. D. (1983). *The value of facing a challenge.* La Jolla, CA: Value Communications.

Keats, E. J. (1967). *Peter's chair.* New York: Harper & Row.

Mann, P. (1971). *My dad lives in a downtown hotel.* New York: Avalon Books.

Ramsey, R. W. (1985). *A lady, a champion.* Wheaton, IL: Tyndale Publishers.

Redl, F., & Wineman, D. (1951). *Children who hate.* New York: Free Press.

Silverstein, S. (1981). *A light in the attic.* New York: HarperCollins.

U.S. Department of Education. (2000). *To assure the free and appropriate public education of children with disabilities: Twenty-second annual report to Congress on the implementation of the Individuals with Disabilities Education Act.* Washington, DC: Author.

Yolen, J. (1990). *Sky dogs.* San Diego: Harcourt Brace Jovanovich.

Solving Social Problems 10

All students are challenged by interpersonal problems, but troubled youngsters, in particular, have chronic problems with relationships. They seem trapped in patterns of behavior that keep them stuck in negative ways of relating to others. Their lack of flexibility in managing their social lives causes them hardship. They are unable to move beyond an unpleasant event and focus on present concerns. They cannot apply lessons from past experience to current interpersonal exchanges. They fail to anticipate the consequences of their behavior, and they are unable to resolve conflicts.

FOCUSING ON THE PRESENT

Learning to let go of an unpleasant event and go on with the normal routine of the school day is beyond the capabilities of some students. Nicholas Long (1992), reporting data from select day-treatment programs for troubled children, indicated that approximately 20% of all serious behavior difficulties occur in the first 40 minutes of the day. Many of these are carryovers from home or community events.

David was such a student. Each morning's bus ride to school was a test for David. The 45-minute trip with eight of his peers often was the catalyst for a crisis at school. Once agitated, it would take David (and me) most of the day to get him composed and focused on his schoolwork. David was unable to monitor or control his own behavior, and he was unaware of how his feelings connected to his actions.

Initially, students like David need the opportunity to discuss such feelings as anger, jealousy, or vengefulness without fear of retribution. They need to ventilate negative feelings, so they can then go on with their day.

Students who have difficulty focusing on the present need a classroom structure that helps them separate feelings from behavior. This requires good models and learning activities that highlight the connections between feelings and actions.

LEARNING FROM PAST EXPERIENCE

Applying lessons from the past is a basic tool for improving interpersonal skills. Many troubled youngsters seem oblivious to the lessons to be learned from either past successes or failures. They continue to make the same mistakes in their relationships over and over again.

Nathaniel was a lonely 12-year-old. Each day at recess, he would wander around the playground by himself, watching other students play. He spent a lot of his time sitting by the schoolyard fence. The other kids kept their distance from Nathaniel for good reasons. His strange ways of trying to make personal contact kept them at a distance. Sometimes he would hide behind a door and frighten the first person, usually a girl, who walked into the room. Nathaniel pinched and poked kids who walked in line with him. He teased and bullied younger children. Nathaniel was an unhappy child, and his unhappiness infected his behavior.

Nathaniel was unable to change his unproductive ways of relating to other children. He believed the other kids were unfair or selfish. He saw his own behavior as justifiable retribution for their inattention. He saw himself as a victim. Nathaniel was a deeply troubled youngster trapped in a cycle of damaged relationships.

Young people like Nathaniel have a cognitive deficit that has stunted their emotional development. The cognitive link between past and present behavior is not established. These students need, first of all, to learn that past experience provides trail markers for future behavior. This is uneven ground, and troubled children are unable to traverse it without an experienced guide.

In much the same way that a creative history teacher helps students relate the past to present events, teachers can help students with troubling behaviors learn that their personal histories contain meaningful lessons. Such classroom activities as personal timelines, activity-based history units, and readings in children's literature help to establish a cognitive link between past and present behavior. Teachers should follow these with such interventions as behavior contracts and Life Space Intervention to personalize their efforts and help their students learn to use past experience to guide future actions.

ANTICIPATING CONSEQUENCES

One of the paradoxes of troubled students is that they persist in disruptive behavior despite unpleasant consequences. Their subjective evaluation of events rarely takes the principle of cause and effect into account. When confronted

SKILL 16: SELECTING TENSION-REDUCING ACTIVITIES

PHASE I

Teach the Concept

Conduct a class discussion about stress. Write the word "stress" on the blackboard and ask students what it means. Responses might include "stressed out" and other expressions with which students are familiar. Emphasize that stress causes tension. Demonstrate with a balloon: "See how the skin of the balloon stretches as more air (stress) is added." Ask students to predict what will happen if you keep blowing into the balloon.

Explain that stress causes tension, and, unless the tension is alleviated, the consequences can be harmful. Ask students if they ever feel tense, and write situations that cause stress on the board. Ask students what they do when they feel stress. Classify responses into harmful and healthful stress reactions. Discuss how such activities as exercise, reading, and playing help reduce stress.

PHASE II

Subskill

To identify physical signs of stress.

Sample Activities

Science

Have students take each other's pulse and record the number of heartbeats in a minute. Then have students do two minutes of calisthenics and measure each other's pulse again. Compare the results. Follow the same routine with a stethoscope.

Mathematics

Students keep a record of their resting and post-exertion pulse rates and calculate the average for a week.

Subskill

To identify situations that cause stress.

Sample Activities

Social Studies

Every major change in history is prompted by social stressors. Discuss the Vietnam War and how demon-

Accept and Acknowledge Feelings	Let students know that it is okay to be frustrated; it is a natural feeling when one is trying to do well.
"Withitness"	At any given moment, at least one or two students are experiencing some frustration with their work. Become adept at identifying these students and attending to them right away.
Positive and Intermittent Reinforcement	Give students incentives to persevere. Emphasize that effort is most important when dealing with frustration.

with negative consequences, troubled youngsters will blame their teachers for picking on them, blame their friends for being mean, or blame their parents for not understanding them.

The teacher who must discipline a troubled student is baffled by the minimal impact of punishment. For instance, the student who habitually belittles classmates would seem to learn that obnoxious behavior has dire consequences in terms of adult and peer retribution. Yet, for troubled students, these negative reactions just serve to strengthen the perception that others are out to get them.

Helping these children make the connection between their behavior and its effects is the challenge. Look for opportunities to discuss cause and effect in class. The notion of cause and effect permeates many curriculum areas, including science, history, and literature.

For example, present scientific experiments that require students to make cause-and-effect predictions. Discuss historical incidents that shaped future events, such as the Emancipation Proclamation and the Declaration of Independence. Encourage students to speculate about the outcomes of characters in stories. Ask them to describe alternative endings. Suggest student essays that are based on imaginary cause-and-effect plots, such as what would happen if the polar ice cap would melt, or what if we woke up in the morning and there was no school. Alternate curriculum activities with role-playing and brainstorming sessions that encourage students to consider consequences of behavior in various situations.

RESOLVING CONFLICTS

Conflict resolution is at the heart of many social-skills programs currently used in public schools. Listening, talking through problems, empathy, and negotiation are basic skills for working through disagreements. These skills can be learned with practice, but not without an overall commitment to community in the classroom. Before students can learn the basic skills of resolving conflict, they must respect the integrity of each individual. Mutual respect makes conflict resolution a worthwhile activity. A meaningful conflict-resolution program fosters attachment, achievement, and autonomy.

Brendtro and Long (1994) describe the conditions that support conflict resolution.

Fostering attachment: The more troubled and "beset" youths are, the more they need close personal attachments in order to reconstruct their lives. These positive bonds should characterize both adult and peer relationships. Programs that do not foster such attachments distance themselves from delinquent youth and thereby have diminished capacity to influence them.

Fostering achievement: *Delinquent behavior is often provoked by school failure. Teachers in successful school programs give students "uncommonly warm emotional support" and prevent them from failing. Youths who become interested in school and make achievement gains have better subsequent community adjustment.*

Fostering autonomy: *Adult domination and authoritarian control fuel negative peer subcultures that sabotage treatment goals. Involving delinquents in decision making, even in highly secure settings, fosters the turn-around to prosocial values and behavior.*

Conflict resolution is practiced under adult supervision, but it is carried out spontaneously, apart from adult intervention. Walking away from a fight, conceding a point during an argument, or ignoring a disrespectful remark requires courage. Youths who are successful in avoiding conflicts may be labeled as lacking in manhood. Worse yet, the youth who walks away from a fight may be targeted for further attacks because he is considered weak. For conflict resolution to take hold, the needs of students on the street, as well as in school, must be taken into account.

The following four units present examples of how to incorporate the self-control skills associated with solving social problems into daily lessons.

SKILL 17: FOCUSING ON PRESENT SITUATIONS

PHASE I

Teach the Concept

Role-play "The Bad Bus Ride." In Scene 1, "On the Bus," a student is riding the bus, and two other students tease him about his haircut. He argues briefly, and he is embarrassed. The two students stop, and the bus ride continues. In Scene 2, "The Classroom," the teased student comes into the classroom in a huff. He slams his books on his desk and says he isn't doing any work. The teacher tries to get him to talk about his feelings, but he puts his head on his desk and ignores the teacher's questions.

In Scene 3, it is recess and the student is too upset to play. His best friend comes over and sits beside him. He talks to his upset friend, and both boys join a game in progress. Ask students watching the role-playing exercise how the teased boy felt. Are there any other ways he could have dealt with his anger when he came into class? Why was he able to join the game after his friend talked to him? Ask actors to report their thoughts about the scenario.

Ask students to describe times when they have been upset and unable to move on to another activity. Help students to acknowledge the difficulties in "letting go" of such feelings as disappointment, frustration, anger, and sadness.

PHASE II

Subskill

To verbalize disturbing feelings.

Sample Activities

Children's Literature

Use books that deal with such themes as divorce, a disability, death of a loved one, losing a best friend, and so on. Make these books available to students during free reading time. Pick selected titles to read aloud and discuss in class. (The use of books to help students deal with feelings is called bibliotherapy.)

Have students keep response journals in which they write down their feelings about specific books.

Social Studies   Many of the major events in history are the result of historic figures choosing to act despite feelings of doubt and fear. Organize students in cooperative groups, assign them a historical event that meets that criterion, and have them write a 10-minute play about it. Each main character should have two scripts: first, the speaking-acting part; and second, the feeling part. An actor speaks, then a student standing behind the actor recites the character's thoughts. Some possibilities include:

- Abraham Lincoln signing the Emancipation Proclamation.

- Muhammad Ali refusing to fight in Vietnam and being stripped of his heavyweight championship.

- Harry S. Truman signing the order to drop the first atomic bomb.

- Rosa Parks refusing to give up her seat on the bus.

Subskill   **To concentrate on a task.**

Sample Activities

Learning Centers   Manipulatives help focus attention. Build frequent hands-on activities into the daily schedule.

Mathematics   Use such manipulative programs as *Mathematics Their Way* (K–2) and *Mathematics: A Way of Thinking* (3–6) (Addison-Wesley).

Computer Programs   Use programs that combine imaginative graphics with skills. Some examples are: *Outnumbered* by The Learning Company (math), *Storybook Weaver* by The Learning Company (writing), and *Where in the U.S.A. Is Carmen Sandiego?* by Broderbund (geography). These and similar programs enhance reading skills as well.

Have the school's computers placed in each classroom, rather than in computer labs.

Across the Curriculum

Be alert to distractions in your classroom. Fix flickering fluorescent lights; set up a quiet area with a partition to block out visual distractions.

Because rocking can help soothe and focus attention, place a rocking chair in the classroom. Play soothing music to help calm students during the beginning of the school day and during transitions.

POSITIVE BEHAVIORAL SUPPORTS

Remove Seductive Objects

Some students have a history of being distracted by objects. Removing these objects helps focus a student.

Life Space Intervention

Encourage students to talk about what is bothering them. Help them formulate a plan for making it through the day.

Hypodermic Affection

Let students know that their feelings are important to you. Emphasize that while you accept their feelings, you cannot allow their behavior to disrupt their or other students' learning.

Reality Appraisal

Point out to students the consequences of their behavior. Ask them to tell you what could happen if they disrupt the classroom.

Direct Appeal

Tell a disruptive student that you are concerned and that, while you would like to talk with the student about the problem, at the moment you are busy with the entire class. Set up a specific time during the day when the two of you can meet to discuss the incident that disturbed the student.

Time-out

This is the last resort. It works best in conjunction with the Life Space Intervention. Otherwise, consider it a cooling-off period, and downplay the punitive aspects.

SKILL 18: LEARNING FROM PAST EXPERIENCE

PHASE I

Teach the Concept

Do a unit on ancient Egypt. Some activities include having students develop their own hieroglyphics, draw or build model pyramids, visit a local museum, or invite a guest speaker who has visited Egypt. Ask students to brainstorm the ways in which the ancient Egyptians contributed to our modern way of life. (This theme could be developed with other cultures.)

Focus students on the notion that we always learn from the past. Use other illustrations to highlight your point from your personal experience. Ask students to describe a lesson they learned from their past experience (for example, after getting sunburned, learning to wear sunscreen to the beach). Make a chart divided into two sides. On the left side, list "events" (without using student names); on the right side, list "lessons learned." Post the chart in the classroom; refer to it regularly, and expand on it as students think of new ideas to contribute.

PHASE II

Subskill

To describe a chronology of events.

Sample Activities

Language Arts

Read aloud an interesting story, then organize students into cooperative-learning groups. Give each group art materials and have the group illustrate the most important events in the story. The group should organize their drawings by sequencing them according to the story line. Share the drawings with the class.

History

Select a unit from a social studies text. Have students work in pairs to construct timelines for the unit. Each timeline should identify key events and dates.

146

Subskill	To learn from the experience of others.

Sample Activities

Social Studies   For elementary students, bring newspaper articles that provide a lesson in living. For example, a golfer gets struck by lightning, or a family's home burns because there are no smoke detectors. Look for articles about local good Samaritans. Display the articles on the bulletin board.

Provide students with copies of old newspapers. Organize them in cooperative learning groups and have each group find news stories that provide a lesson in living.

Language Arts   For primary students, read *The Big Pile of Dirt* by Eleanor Clymer. Ask students to describe what they learned from the story. Follow up with other books, and continue to emphasize lessons to be learned from the lives and acts of others.

For elementary students, have them write a letter to an admired individual. Have the students describe the qualities the individual has that the students admire.

Subskill	To learn from one's own experience.

Sample Activities

Brainstorming   Ask students to name things that other youngsters do that make them upset. Do not allow names or blame. List the behavior on the blackboard. Have the students decide on a behavior that would be positive and opposite to the upsetting behavior. Make a paper chain with each student's name and the positive behavior that he or she is committed to putting into action for the week. Each day, have a follow-up discussion to talk about progress.

Across the Curriculum   Make a pride line. On the line, write or draw events about which the students are proud. Some examples are:

- things I've done for family or friends
- schoolwork

- how I've earned money

- good habits

- things I've shared

- successes I've had

Each student discusses the pride line with a partner, including as much information as possible. Students come together as a group and each student is introduced by the partner, who names things that make the student special.

POSITIVE BEHAVIORAL SUPPORTS

Life Space Intervention

Each intervention session should highlight the pattern of a student's behavior. As a student becomes more aware of how she or he typically reacts in a conflict situation, the value of using past experience will become more obvious. Emphasize that learning from past mistakes is a critical social problem-solving skill.

Show Personal Interest

A trusting relationship helps students change their behavior. Emphasize that it is student actions and not the person that is the issue in discipline problems.

Positive Reinforcement

During the initial stages of behavior change, a student may need social or tangible rewards to stay on the right track. Intermittent reinforcers work best.

Behavior Contracts

These signed statements keep behavior-change agreements on track. Using the contract as a reminder supports student efforts by relating past commitments to present behavior.

SKILL 19: ANTICIPATING CONSEQUENCES

PHASE I

Teach the Concept Present the class with the following situations:

- A child forgets to feed her pet guinea pig.

- Youngsters climb on a garage roof after they have been warned to stay off.

- A teenager is caught shoplifting.

- A child puts her arm in a bear cage at the zoo.

- A child borrows a toy and decides to keep it.

- A student goes to the mall instead of doing homework.

- A child is always chosen last during recess games.

Primary-age children can respond in a large group. Elementary children can brainstorm answers together in small groups and record their responses to report to the entire class. These situations can be modified to fit events that relate to students' lives. Discuss the meaning of the word "consequences." For a follow-up game, play "consequences jeopardy." Write some consequences on index cards, and see how many causes students can come up with.

PHASE II

Subskill To explain cause and effect.

Sample Activities

Language Arts For elementary children, read *Tom's Midnight Garden* by A. Phillippa Pearce. Discuss the themes of actions and consequences.

For primary students, read *No Jumping on the Bed* by Tedd Arnold. Discuss how actions can lead to bad effects.

Science Conduct various demonstrations and ask students to predict the effects. For example, drop different-size objects; place a glass over a burning candle; put objects made of different materials in a tub of water; or mix various food colors.

Subskill   **To understand the meaning of consequences.**

Sample Activities

Language Arts   For primary students, read *The Night the Toys Had a Party* by Enid Blyton. Discuss the consequences of Ben's behavior.

For elementary students, read *Just A Dream* by Chris Van Allsburg. Discuss the potential consequences of pollution.

For both primary and elementary students, read "Sarah Cynthia Sylvia Stout Would Not Take the Garbage Out" from Shel Silverstein's *Where the Sidewalk Ends*. Have students discuss their chores at home and the consequences of ignoring their responsibilities.

Social Studies   Organize students in cooperative-learning groups. Have each group come up with consequences for the following scenarios:

- The British win the Revolutionary War.

- The South wins the Civil War.

- The ozone layer is depleted more each year.

- Schools decide to stop using grades to evaluate students.

- A live Tyrannosaurus Rex is discovered in Zaire.

- Radio astronomers pick up signals indicating intelligent life in a distant galaxy.

- Girls are not allowed to play basketball or softball.

- It is illegal for parents to punish their children.

Subskill   **To accept consequences for behavior.**

Sample Activities

Peer Review   Establish a peer review for classroom infractions. A student pleads his or her own case. The teacher presents evidence. And the class uses a secret ballot to determine the student's guilt. Sanctions are predetermined, but another student can plead for leniency. The class would again use a secret ballot to determine if leniency is granted.

Class Discussion   The class works together to determine the sanctions for typical classroom discipline violations.

Social Studies   Invite a guest speaker who is familiar with the legal system. Police officers, judges, ex-gang members, and parole officers are examples. Ask the visitor to describe life in juvenile detention centers and prisons. Arrange a field trip to a local jail or juvenile detention center.

POSITIVE BEHAVIORAL SUPPORTS

Life Space Intervention   The student develops a plan for dealing with the behavior incident that led to the Life Space Intervention. Provide supportive statements to help the student prepare for consequences for misbehavior. Wood and Long (1991) suggest the following:

- "What will you do if . . ."

- "What if he doesn't listen?"

- "It will be hard to say no to your friends when they try that again. What will you do?"

- "The next time they tell you to do that, you are going to feel just as angry. What will happen?"

Sane Messages   Provide feedback about behavior that is disturbing, why the behavior is disturbing, and the behavior you would like to see. For example: "Alex, your talking during quiet reading time is distracting me and other students. If you are finished, select another book." This statement helps students to recognize that their behavior affects others, and it underscores the need to select nondisruptive alternatives.

Logical Consequences   If a student makes a mess, he or she must clean it up. A student who is late for class must make up missed work. A student who does not complete homework must finish it during free time. A student who bullies or teases during recess stays in for 2 days. Logical consequences provide sanctions that match the infraction. When it seems appropriate, ask students to determine logical consequences for their misbehavior. Keep in mind that the purpose is not to punish but to help students to reflect on the consequences of their behavior.

Reality Appraisal

Pushing a student can cause an injury. If you tease a friend, you could lose a playmate. If you are disobedient, your parent might punish you. Reinforce the notion that in life there are consequences for misbehavior. In your classroom, all students require limits. They need to know that they are safe. Setting limits means clearly stating expected behavior, what is unacceptable, and why.

SKILL 20: RESOLVING CONFLICTS

PHASE I

Teach the Concept

Read "The Toad and the Kangaroo" from *A Light in the Attic* by Shel Silverstein (1981). Why were the toad and the kangaroo unable to get along? Explain that the word "conflict" often is used to describe arguments that do not get settled.

In a group discussion, ask students if they sometimes have conflicts with friends. Ask them to name some of the things about which they argue with their friends. List "conflict points" on the board. Select one conflict point and ask two students to role-play the situation. During the role play, use the freeze technique. Stop the characters by saying "freeze" at points where misunderstandings or intensity appears to be causing the conflict to escalate. Ask the characters why they are acting that way. Ask specific questions, such as "What do you think the other person is feeling now?" Videotape this and other conflict role plays. After the role play, ask students to brainstorm how the situation could have been resolved amicably.

PHASE II

Subskill

To recognize conflict situations.

Sample Activities

Children's Literature

For primary students, read *The Tears of the Dragon* by Hirusuke Hamada. Discuss how prejudice influences people's behavior.

For elementary students, read *The Bully of Barkham Street* by Mary Stoltz. Stop the story at various points and ask students to describe how they believe the conflicts could be resolved.

Art

Start a comic-strip conflict by drawing a scenario on the first two panels of a five-panel cartoon. Use large sheets of paper. Have students in small groups draw a resolution to the conflict. (Adapted from Priscilla

Prutzman, "Creative Conflict Resolution," in *Learning,* March 1994, pp. 47–49.)

Subskill   To develop alternatives to conflict.

Sample Activities

Social Studies   Bring in newspaper articles about conflict in foreign countries. Use maps to help students identify places that are in conflict. Ask youngsters to discuss how these conflicts could be resolved.

Make a "situation board," using the bulletin board. Students determine conflicts that go on the board. Use maps and art materials to highlight conflict "hot spots."

Language Arts   Write a letter to a Congressperson, mayor, or some other politician with suggestions for resolving a specific conflict that students have identified on their "situation board."

Subskill   To use words to resolve conflicts.

Sample Activities

Across the Curriculum   Conflicts can come up at any time during the school day. Explain to students that the following Win/Win Guidelines will be used for all student conflicts. Post these guidelines:

1. Take time for cooling off. Find alternative ways to express anger.

2. Each person states their feelings and the problem as they see it, using "I" messages. No blaming, no name-calling, no interrupting.

3. Each person states the problem as the other person sees it.

4. Each person says how they themselves are responsible for their problem.

5. Brainstorm solutions together and choose a solution that satisfies both—a Win/Win solution.

6. Affirm your partner.

(From *Learning the Skills of Peacemaking* by Naomi Drew, 1987; pp. 31–39.)

Award peacemaker badges to students who work to resolve conflicts. To win a badge, a student has to be nominated by an adult or child who witnessed the peacemaker resolving a conflict.

Language Arts — Have students keep personal journals in which they write for 10 minutes each day. Encourage students to write about personal problems, worries, and conflicts. Explain that writing helps one work through feelings and develop solutions. These journals are private. Keep them locked up between entries. Students can share journal entries on a voluntary basis.

Social Studies — Place students in cooperative-learning groups. Assign each group a famous peacemaker. Some examples include Gandhi, Albert Schweitzer, Mother Teresa, Martin Luther King, Jr., and Nelson Mandela. Have each group develop a peacemaker display, including books, pictures, posters, important facts, and so on. Exhibit displays in the classroom.

POSITIVE BEHAVIORAL SUPPORTS

Modeling — Students will watch the way you handle conflict in the classroom. There are many ways to defuse conflicts between yourself and students. Some of those mentioned in this book include hypodermic affection, humor, accepting and acknowledging feelings, negotiating, behavior contracts, and "I" messages. Avoid power struggles. Keep in mind the conflict cycle depicted in Chapter 4. Remember that your response to student misbehavior can inadvertently accelerate the conflict cycle by adding more stress to the situation.

Life Space Intervention — This behavior-management approach was developed specifically to help deal with crisis situations. It helps make you a better listener, while helping students accept responsibility for their behavior. For more information about Life Space Intervention, see Mary M. Wood and Nicholas J. Long, *Life Space Intervention: Talking with Children and Youth in Crisis,* 1993.

REFERENCES

Arnold, T. (1987). *No jumping on the bed.* New York: Dial.

Blyton, E. (1989). *The night the toys had a party.* New York: Gallery Books.

Brendtro, L. K., & Long, N. J. (1994). Violence begets violence: Breaking conflict cycles. *Journal of Emotional and Behavioral Problems, 3*(1), 2–7.

Clymer, E. (1968). *The big pile of dirt.* New York: Holt, Rinehart, & Winston.

Drew, N. (1987). *Learning the skills of peacemaking.* Rolling Hills Estate, CA: Jalmar Press.

Hamada, H. (1967). *The tears of the dragon.* New York: Parents Magazine Press.

Long, N. J. (1992). Crisis as opportunity: Looking beyond behavior and seeing my needs: A red flag interview. *Journal of Emotional and Behavioral Problems, 1*(2), 35–38.

Pearce, A. P. (1986). *Tom's midnight garden.* New York: Dell.

Silverstein, S. (1974). *Where the sidewalk ends.* New York: Harper & Row.

Silverstein, S. (1981). *A light in the attic.* New York: HarperCollins.

Stoltz, M. (1985). *The bully of Barkham Street.* New York: HarperCollins.

Van Allsburg, C. (1990). *Just a dream.* Boston: Houghton Mifflin.

Wood, M. M., & Long, N. J. (1991). *Life space intervention: Talking with children and youth in crisis.* Austin, TX: Pro-Ed.

Resiliency

11

Troubled young people have more right with them than wrong about them. This simple but powerful fact is easy to overlook, because what is wrong draws so much of our attention. It is hard to appreciate the artistic talent of a 12-year-old girl whose idea of conflict resolution is a swipe with a razor. It is equally difficult to see the budding young poet in the 10-year-old who does most of his writing with a spray can. Spotting the business acumen in a 13-year-old drug dealer requires a stretch of insight that few possess.

Some youngsters have had more negative experiences in their first 10 years than many of us will have in a lifetime. Their case histories are different, but how they adapt is similar. They develop hard outer shells to protect themselves from further pain. This character armor is intended to resist change in order to keep their world predictable and manageable. Their emotional development stagnates because the energy they need for growth is sidetracked into dead-end defense mechanisms, such as denial, projection, and rationalization.

The actions of troubled students are dictated by whatever bundle of misperceptions they bring to bear on a situation. It is these misperceptions that guide their behavior. Their actions are controlled more by feelings than by logic. As Fritz Redl pointed out: "There is a difference between having feelings and being had by your feelings. If your feelings flood you, then your behavior becomes out of control" (Wood & Long, 1991).

Picking out the social abilities possessed by troubled youngsters is hard, because their dysfunctional behavior demands so much attention. The problem is compounded by the labels used to describe troubled children. Such terms as "oppositional defiant disorder," "conduct disorder," and "attention deficit hyperactivity disorder" are intimidating and serve to underscore the pathological aspects of a youngster's social skills. (American Psychiatric Association, 2000). Even worse, the labels can undermine a child's faith in himself or herself.

In special education, they call this "learned helplessness." If we believe students are unable to change, we will communicate this to them, and in so doing, we help establish a self-fulfilling cycle of failure. Nothing brings hope screeching to a halt faster than negative expectations do.

But students are not always as they are advertised. If you concentrate as much on what a student is doing right as on what he or she is doing wrong, you construct a fuller account of his or her capabilities.

Concentrate on self-control abilities, as well as weaknesses. This positive approach will communicate your faith that every child has the capacity to overcome life's hurdles. You will never know for sure who among your students will make it or who will not. This is the occupational hazard of teaching—we rarely see the products of our labors. However, the research on resiliency in children underscores the importance of a strong, caring mentor as a key factor in their ability to rise above demanding childhoods to become competent adults.

In 1960, Robert Coles, a young psychiatrist, was driving in New Orleans when he found his way blocked by a milling crowd. When he got out of his car to investigate, he became a witness to a historic moment. He saw a 6-year-old African-American girl, dressed in her best white dress, on her way to school. Ruby Bridges, her head held high, needed an escort of federal marshals to guide her through a jeering mob of white parents. They threw tomatoes at her, and they called her "nigger."

Ruby was the first black child to break the color barrier in the New Orleans public school system. The contrast between the stoic dignity of the little girl and the crowd of racists who taunted her made a lifelong impression on Coles. (It also was the inspiration for one of Norman Rockwell's best-known paintings.) His curiosity was piqued by the courage of such a young child. Coles wanted to understand how a solitary child could muster the courage to calmly face such an ordeal. His interviews with Ruby and other children became the basis for his life work, which includes *Children of Crisis: A Study of Courage and Fear* (1964) and *The Moral Life of Children* (1986).

In his writings, Coles' thinking evolved from psychiatric interpretations of his young subjects to highlighting the power of human attachment and moral values as a cornerstone of resiliency. Recently, Ruby Bridges Hall, child advocate, was reading an account of her struggle to integrate William Frantz Elementary School to a group of children. She paused to ask the children what they can do to be brave.

"I just tell myself I can do anything I want," one boy responded.

"Yes," Mrs. Hall said, "You do have to talk to yourself a lot" (Judson, 1995).

We all "talk to ourselves a lot." Our internal dialogue influences our behavior in many ways. We worry; we plan; we resolve to do better. But what about the internal dialogue of troubled children? What mental resources do they have to fall back on in times of stress?

We can never have direct access to children's secret thoughts, but we can ask them what they think. We might not always like what we hear, but the information they give us is crucial in understanding their behavior. All of us, young people included, are continually interpreting the world around us, and it is these interpretations that guide behavior. If we want to understand why troubled youngsters behave as they do, we need to listen to their voices.

Daniel Way is a 15-year-old student at a therapeutic school in Cleveland. In a two-page essay, Daniel described some of his thoughts about his behavior and the way he is treated:

> *Sometimes its like I just have a half heart. I don't feel pain*
> *sometimes. I don't feel sorry. I just have a half heart. One half*
> *of me that feels is for my girlfriend. That's the ONLY part that*
> *feels. The other part don't give a damn. Because the more I try,*
> *the more sh-- the crackers come up with to try to rob me of my*
> *right to every damn thing I want in life. And this has been*
> *going on all through school since kindergarten. Every f---ing*
> *cracker lies and tries to take my respect and manhood. You*
> *have no idea what it's like to be a Black man. They're scared*
> *if you have just one ounce of manliness, so they always trying*
> *to persecute you and put you down.* (1993, p. 5)

Recently, I asked a group of young people who are in a special education program for behavior disorders to write down something about themselves. This is what Reynaldo, age 10, had to say:

> *What I like about myself is when I see strangers who offer me*
> *candy or who I see around that I don't know. I live in one of*
> *the dangerous places in the world and nothing bad happen to*
> *me yet.*

Daniel and Reynaldo are troubled youth. Each has misperceptions about themselves and others that have landed them in special education programs. But each also has an inner strength that bolsters their resilience to the difficulties that surround them. The resilience of youth is their greatest asset.

The first time I saw Jerome, I thought there was something special about him. Although average height for his age, his sturdiness made him appear bigger and more mature. Unless provoked, he was quiet, almost dignified, in his demeanor. While other kids swaggered, Jerome strolled. He had no need for facades; Jerome was the real deal. We had some tough kids in the school, but nobody messed with Jerome.

Jerome's cumulative folder told the tale of a kid going nowhere. He read three years below grade level, and about once a month he would tangle with someone—a teacher, an instructional aide, the principal, and, on a few occasions, other kids. But the latter was the exception; and, when he did get into a fight with another kid, it usually was an older student who, like the movie gunslinger, would confront Jerome to find out just how tough he was. Jerome's disruptions in school were never minor; most of them usually ended with a suspension.

Jerome had many misperceptions about teachers and school. Primarily, he believed that teachers did not like him. His understanding was based on reality as he experienced it. School for Jerome was a litany of failure. His academic deficiencies haunted him every day. His confidence in his ability to learn in school and succeed in life had bottomed out long before we met. Despite his shortcomings, it did not take long for me to admire Jerome's resiliency. He did not back down from anybody, and, among the other students, he was a natural leader.

One week, his teacher was absent, and the principal, Mr. McEntee, assigned me to substitute. My entrance signaled wonderful possibilities for the 25 fifth-graders, who knew a fun opportunity when they saw it. The dreaded greeting, "Yeah, a sub," welcomed me as I walked into the classroom on Monday morning. I asked Jerome to step out into the hall with me. Outside the range of the other students, I told Jerome I wanted him to be my first lieutenant. Whenever I directed the students, he would be my backup. It was a calculated risk, but Jerome never bullied, and I felt he would respond favorably to the responsibility. For the rest of the week, Jerome was my ace in the hole. If the students got rambunctious, a quiet "settle down" from Jerome got everybody's attention. I marveled at Jerome's ability to control the class without intimidation and without generating resentment. It was clear that all the kids respected Jerome.

Jerome had the capacity to lead, but he did not trust adults, particularly white adults. When pushed, he would push back, and this was the source of many of his school discipline problems. Jerome and I spent a lot of time together outside of school. He taught me about resilience, and I taught him how to read. Whenever I hear someone describe a child as a "loser" or a "troublemaker," I think of Jerome.

The ability of many youngsters to weather difficult childhoods and go on to successful lives is well documented. In a 30-year longitudinal study, four researchers, Emmy E. Werner, Ruth S. Smith, Jessie M. Bierman, and Fern E. French (cited in Burger, 1994), followed the development of 698 children born in 1955 on the Hawaiian island of Kauai. Their objective was to assess and document the effects of adverse conditions on children's development. The researchers paid particular interest to a group of 201 high-risk children. As they matured, two-thirds of the youngsters in the high-risk group developed behavior and learning problems. Their case histories revealed such dysfunctional parental patterns as alcoholism, mental illness, and abuse. Despite the same developmental setbacks, approximately one-third of the high-risk population became competent young adults.

An analysis of the temperaments of the children who succeeded reveals that many had such qualities as humor, warmth, and flexibility that ingratiated them to their peers and adults. They were active learners who solved problems and concentrated on their school work. Joseph Burger (1994) underscored the value of this study to teachers of troubled students when he reported, "The investigators felt that if other children could be taught how to develop these qualities, they too might become more resilient when faced with adverse conditions."

Three environmental factors contribute to the development of resiliency in youth:

MENTOR RELATIONSHIPS

A mentor relationship is a critical element in a youth's ability to persevere in the face of despair. A trusting relationship with an adult who nurtures the positive attributes of a child serves as a model for developing other healthy relationships.

Adolescents, in particular, need at least one adult who will accept their propensity for rebellion and argument, without responding in kind. As Virginia Rezmierski (1987) noted when considering the issue of discipline with youth, "it is probably more important to think about the nature of the hand inside the glove, how mature it is, rather than to think about the steel or the velvet." When one is developing a relationship with a troubled youth, conflicts are inevitable. Effective mentors model the behaviors they want to see children develop.

SCHOOL ACTIVITIES

School activities that promote success help develop confidence. Meaningful school activities take student needs and life experiences into account. Such lessons emphasize the connection between academic skills and life outside of school. Lessons that students see as meaningful provide an infrastructure for preventing classroom disturbances and supporting self-control. Disinterest and frustration with dull lessons elicits disruptive behavior.

Schoolwork that promotes creative expression helps troubled youth find outlets for their anger and frustration. Music, drama, writing, arts, crafts, and dance enable youngsters to explore their feelings and uncover hidden talents.

COMMUNITY PROGRAMS

Community programs demonstrate to youth that there is a network of adults who are concerned with their welfare, and community programs provide opportunities for troubled youth to mingle with a wide range of young people and adults. The increased exposure to positive role models is one of the strongest assets of community programs. The African proverb, "It takes a village to raise a child," is a fitting reminder of the value of community programs for troubled youth.

The Omega Boys Club in San Francisco uses a combination of mentoring and peer counseling to teach at-risk youngsters to become contributing members of their community. It has helped 108 Omega members enroll in college, and Omega offers an employment training program for non-college-bound youth. More than 500 youngsters have become members of Omega. Many of them enlisted while placed in juvenile detention centers.

Another example of effective community action is the Community Youth Gang Service in Los Angeles. This highly successful program is a partnership between police, public schools, and other community organizations. Outreach members patrol high-crime neighborhoods. Several gang truces are attributed to the efforts of CYGS outreach teams. The economic needs of youth are met by a job development component, which matches ex-gang members and employers.

Emotional development is nurtured by positive feedback, companionship, and fulfilling relationships. Disruptive and violent students need to learn new ways of viewing their behavior and their relationships. The payoffs are enriched relationships with peers and adults, improved self-concept, and better school performance.

The Self-Control Curriculum provides an educational impetus for resiliency. By helping to teach your students how to control impulses, follow school routines, manage stress, solve social problems, and participate in groups, you will help them gain the social skills they need to join mainstream society.

The recommendations in this book are just starting points. You need to decide what your priorities are. A television commercial once extolled people to practice preventive maintenance on their cars by saying, "You can pay me now, or you can pay me later." The same holds true for the Self-Control Curriculum. You can deal with the same behavior problems, day in and day out, or you can do something about them by teaching students the self-control skills they need for success in your classroom. An emphasis on self-control development may take more time up front, but the gains will be well worth the investment, both for you and your students.

REFERENCES

American Psychiatric Association (2000). *Diagnostic and statistical manual of mental disorders DSM-IV-TR (text revision)*. Washington, DC: Author.

Burger, J. V. (1994). "Keys to resilience: Highlights in resilience research." *Journal of Emotional and Behavioral Problems, 3*(2), 6–10.

Coles, R. (1967). *Children of crisis: A study of courage and fear*. Boston: Little, Brown.

Coles, R. (1986). *The moral life of children*. Boston: Houghton Mifflin.

Judson, G. (1995). "Child of courage joins her biographer." *New York Times,* September 1, pp. B1, B5.

Rezmierski, V. E. (1987). "Discipline: Neither the steel glove nor the velvet, but the maturity inside the glove, that makes the difference." *The Pointer, 31*(4), 5–13.

Way, D. (1993). "I just have a half heart." *Journal of Emotional and Behavioral Problems, 2*(1), 4–5.

Wood, M. M., & Long, N. J. (1991). *Life space intervention: Talking with children and youth in crisis*. Austin, TX: Pro-Ed.

Self-Control Inventory

Student_____ Age_____

Date _____ Rater _____

Class _____ School_____

SELF-CONTROL INVENTORY (SCI)

MARTIN HENLEY, PH.D.

The Self-Control Inventory is a functional guide for assessing student self-control abilities and organizing a self-control curriculum.

Directions: Follow rating procedures described in the manual (see Chapter 2). Transfer student ratings to summary rating below for quick access to student overall self-control skills.

SELF-CONTROL INVENTORY SUMMARY RATING

IMPULSE	SCHOOL ROUTINE	GROUP PRESSURE	STRESS	PROBLEM SOLVING
1. M/S _____	5. F/R _____	9. M/C_____	13. A/N_____	17. F/R_____
2. D/P _____	6. O/M _____	10. A/P _____	14. C/C _____	18. L/E _____
3. V/F _____	7. A/E _____	11. P/G _____	15. T/F _____	19. A/C _____
4. R/O _____	8. C/T _____	12. U/B _____	16. S/A _____	20. R/C _____

GOAL: TO CONTROL IMPULSES

Self-Control Skill	Example

1. ☐ **MANAGES SITUATIONAL LURE**

Student resists the impulse to act out (e.g., shout, run, hit people or objects) in such unstructured spaces outside the classroom as hallways, cafeteria, and field trips.

Student attends a school assembly without becoming overstimulated.

COMMENTS:

Sample Behavioral Objective—*In settings outside the classroom, student maintains composure without teacher intervention.*

2. ☐ **DEMONSTRATES PATIENCE**

Student adapts to normal classroom procedures that require waiting or taking turns.

Student raises hand for help and waits for teacher assistance.

COMMENTS:

Sample Behavioral Objective—*When confronted with a delay in an activity, student waits without teacher reminders.*

3. ☐ **VERBALIZES FEELINGS**

Student verbalizes, rather than acts out feelings.

During a private discussion with the teacher, student expresses disappointment and anger.

COMMENTS:

Sample Behavioral Objective—*During a classroom discussion, student verbalizes feelings with teacher support.*

4. ☐ **RESISTS TEMPTING OBJECTS**

Student resists temptation to misuse objects in situations that could lead to negative consequences.

Student uses ruler for measuring rather than banging on desk.

COMMENTS:

Sample Behavioral Objective—*When given manipulative learning materials, student uses them for their intended purpose without teacher reminders.*

| 1 | rarely | 2 | sometimes | 3 | often | 4 | mastery | n/a | not applicable | n/o | not observable |

GOAL: TO FOLLOW SCHOOL ROUTINES

Self-Control Skill	**Example**
5. ☐ **FOLLOWS RULES** Student accepts clearly stated classroom limits.	*When asked by the teacher to work quietly, student complies.* COMMENTS:
Sample Behavioral Objective—*When asked to follow classroom rules, student obeys without teacher reminders.*	
6. ☐ **ORGANIZES SCHOOL MATERIALS** Student keeps track of items needed for school, such as eyeglasses, gym clothes, and pencils.	*Student remembers homework assignments.* COMMENTS:
Sample Behavioral Objective—*During classroom activities, student keeps materials organized.*	
7. ☐ **ACCEPTS EVALUATIVE COMMENTS** Student listens to positive or negative feedback and guides actions accordingly.	*Student uses teacher feedback on math assignments to solve computational problems.* COMMENTS:
Sample Behavioral Objective—*After teacher feedback, student responds appropriately within an acceptable time frame.*	
8. ☐ **MAKES CLASSROOM TRANSITIONS** During the change of lessons or activities within the classroom, student follows classroom procedures.	*Student puts away reading materials and begins working at math activity table.* COMMENTS:
Sample Behavioral Objective—*During transition times, student follows classroom routines with minimal teacher intervention.*	

1 rarely 2 sometimes 3 often 4 mastery n/a not applicable n/o not observable

GOAL: TO MANAGE GROUP SITUATIONS

Self-Control Skill	Example

9. ☐ **MAINTAINS COMPOSURE**
Student maintains control when other students are agitated or excited.

During a classroom activity, student ignores disturbing behaviors of others.

COMMENTS:

Sample Behavioral Objective—*When other class members are disruptive, student maintains self-control with minimal prompting.*

10. ☐ **APPRAISES PEER PRESSURE**
When exposed to peer value judgments or actions, the student selects an individual course of action.

Student refuses to join in with classmates who are teasing a new student.

COMMENTS:

Sample Behavioral Objective—*In a group discussion, the student expresses individual opinions without seeking peer approval.*

11. ☐ **PARTICIPATES IN GROUP ACTIVITY**
Student demonstrates such social group skills as contributing ideas, listening to others, and offering positive feedback.

While working on a group project, student assists other members.

COMMENTS:

Sample Behavioral Objective—*During a cooperative-learning activity, student helps the group achieve goals with minimal teacher intervention.*

12. ☐ **UNDERSTANDS HOW BEHAVIOR AFFECTS OTHERS**
Student verbalizes how behavior or comments can produce a positive or negative reaction in other students.

Student acknowledges that an insult hurt another student's feelings.

COMMENTS:

Sample Behavioral Objective—*After tutoring a peer, student discusses positive effects of helping role with limited teacher prodding.*

1 rarely 2 sometimes 3 often 4 mastery n/a not applicable n/o not observable

GOAL: TO MANAGE STRESS

Self-Control Skill | Example

13. ☐ **ADAPTS TO NEW SITUATIONS**
Student adapts to changes in class personnel, schedule, or routine without withdrawing or acting out problems.

Student accepts a substitute teacher.

COMMENTS:

Sample Behavioral Objective—*Confronted with a change in regular classroom routine, student makes adjustments with minimal teacher assistance.*

14. ☐ **COPES WITH COMPETITION**
Student participates in competitive activities or games without giving up or boasting.

Student continues to enjoy a game when on the losing side.

COMMENTS:

Sample Behavioral Objective—*In a competitive situation, the student participates with minimal teacher support.*

15. ☐ **TOLERATES FRUSTRATION**
Student manages moderate amounts of frustration or disappointment within the classroom.

When a field trip is canceled due to bad weather, student accepts setback and continues with day's activities.

COMMENTS:

Sample Behavioral Objective—*When confronted with a frustrating situation, the student perseveres with teacher support.*

16. ☐ **SELECTS TENSION-REDUCING ACTIVITIES**
When confronted with a stressful situation, student alleviates tension through activities such as games, play, exercise, or other stress-reducing endeavors.

Student who is having a bad day relaxes by playing a favorite game during free time.

COMMENTS:

Sample Behavioral Objective—*Given some options, student participates in stress-reducing activity with minimal teacher prompting.*

[1] rarely [2] sometimes [3] often [4] mastery [n/a] not applicable [n/o] not observable

GOAL: TO SOLVE SOCIAL PROBLEMS

Self-Control Skill	Example

17. ☐ **FOCUSES ON THE PRESENT**

Student rebounds from an unsettling prior experience and concentrates on present tasks.

Student regains composure in classroom after an altercation on the school bus.

COMMENTS:

Sample Behavioral Objective—*After an unpleasant experience, the student regains composure with minimal teacher support.*

18. ☐ **LEARNS FROM PAST EXPERIENCE**

Student uses past mistakes or accomplishments to guide here-and-now decisions.

Student refrains from fighting because a prior incident led to getting in trouble.

COMMENTS:

Sample Behavioral Objective—*Following a discussion about a pattern of classroom disruptions, the student develops and follows an alternative plan for behavior with teacher guidance.*

19. ☐ **ANTICIPATES CONSEQUENCES**

Student refrains from disruptive behavior because of anticipated loss of privilege.

After a reminder that annoying other students means loss of recess, student resumes individual assignment.

COMMENTS:

Sample Behavioral Objective—*When reminded of a negative consequence for actions, student changes behavior without further teacher comment.*

20. ☐ **RESOLVES CONFLICTS**

Student appraises misunderstandings or conflicts and seeks alternative solutions.

Rather than fighting, student negotiates a satisfactory settlement to a dispute.

COMMENTS:

Sample Behavioral Objective—*During a classroom disagreement, student helps work out a compromise with minimal teacher assistance.*

| 1 | rarely | 2 | sometimes | 3 | often | 4 | mastery | n/a | not applicable | n/o | not observable |

Student
Self-Report Form B

SELF-CONTROL CURRICULUM
STUDENT SELF-REPORT FORM

NAME _____   AGE _____

SCHOOL _____   DATE _____

STUDENT STATEMENT	ALWAYS	OFTEN	SOME-TIMES	RARELY
1. I follow school rules outside the classroom.				
2. I wait my turn.				
3. I talk about my feelings.				
4. I use materials correctly.				
5. I follow classroom rules.				
6. I come to class prepared to do my schoolwork.				
7. I accept teacher feedback about the way I behave in class.				
8. I change activities without problems.				
9. I behave in the classroom when other students do not.				
10. I listen to my friends, but I make up my own mind.				
11. I work well during classroom group activities.				
12. I know how my behavior affects others.				
13. I adjust to changes in classroom routines.				
14. I enjoy competitive games.				
15. I keep trying when my work is difficult.				
16. I know how to relax when I am having a bad day.				
17. I don't let one bad experience ruin my day.				
18. I use past experiences to help me decide how to act.				
19. I avoid getting into trouble.				
20. I work out problems with my friends, rather than fighting.				

Comments: _____

_____

_____

PROGRAMA DE AUTO-CONTROL
REPORTE DE LOS ESTUDIANTES

NOMBRE _____ **EDAD** _____

ESCUELA _____ **FECHA** _____

OPINIÓN DEL ESTUDIANTE	SIEMPRE	FRECUENTE-MENTE	ALGUNAS VECES	CASI NUNCA
1. Sigo las reglas de la escuela fuera del salón de clase.				
2. Espero mi turno.				
3. Expreso mis sentimientos bablando.				
4. Uso los materiales correctamente.				
5. Sigo los reglamentos del salón de clase.				
6. Vengo preparado al salón de clase para hacer mi trabajo escolar.				
7. Acepto observaciones de la maestra acerca de mi comportamiento.				
8. Yo cambio de actividades sin ningún problema.				
9. Me comporto bien en el salón de clases aunque otros estudiantes no lo hagan así.				
10. Escucho las opiniones de mis amistades, pero llego a mis propias decisiones.				
11. Trabajo bien en el salón de clase durante grupos de actividades.				
12. Yo sé como mi comportamiento afecta los demás.				
13. Me adapto a los cambios en la rutina diaria del salón de clase.				
14. A mí me gustan los juegos competitivos (competitives).				
15. Sigo tratando cuando el trabajo es dificil.				
16. Sé relajarme cuando tengo un mal día.				
17. No dejo que una mala experiecia eche a perder mi día entero.				
18. Uso mis experiencias para ayudarme a decidir cómo actuar.				
19. Evito meterme en problemas.				
20. Resuelvo los problemas con mis amistades sin tener que pelear.				

Comentarios: _____

_____

_____

Family Report Form

C

SELF-CONTROL CURRICULUM
FAMILY REPORT FORM

STUDENT'S NAME _____ **AGE** _____

SCHOOL _____ **DATE** _____

STUDENT STATEMENT	ALWAYS	OFTEN	SOME-TIMES	RARELY
1. Behaves in unsupervised situations				
2. Is patient				
3. Talks about feelings				
4. Uses toys and other objects appropriately				
5. Follows household rules				
6. Is organized				
7. Accepts feedback about behavior				
8. Follows directions				
9. Is calm when peers are agitated (e.g., avoids arguing)				
10. Considers the effects of peer pressure				
11. Enjoys group activities with other young people				
12. Is aware of how behavior affects others				
13. Adjusts to changes in normal routine				
14. Can cope with competition				
15. Manages frustration				
16. Deals with stress by selecting stress-reducing activities				
17. Regains composure after being angry or upset				
18. Learns from past experiences				
19. Refrains from behaviors that could lead to punishment				
20. Attempts to resolve conflicts without fighting				

Comments: _____

_____

Solution Tree

PROGRAMA DE AUTO-CONTROL
REPORTE DE LA FAMILIA

NOMBRE _____   **EDAD** _____

ESCUELA _____   **FECHA** _____

COMPORTAMIENTO DEL ESTUDIANTE	SIEMPRE	FRECUENTE-MENTE	ALGUNAS VECES	CASI NUNCA
1. Se comporta bien en la ausencia de los padres.				
2. Espera su turno. Tiene paciencia.				
3. Expresa sus sentimientos hablando.				
4. Usa juguetes y otros objetos correctamente.				
5. Sigue las reglas de la casa.				
6. Es organizado bien.				
7. Acepta disciplina acerca de su comportamiento.				
8. Sigue instrucciones.				
9. Se comporta bien aunque otros no lo hagan así. Trata de no disputar.				
10. Escucha las opiniones de sus amistades, pero llega a sus propias decisiones.				
11. Trabaja bien con otros.				
12. Sabe como su comportamiento afecta los demás.				
13. Se adapta a los cambios en la rutina diaria.				
14. Le gustan los juegos competitivos (competitives).				
15. Sigue tratando cuando el trabajo es difícil.				
16. Sabe relajarse cuando está pasando un mal día.				
17. No deja que una mala experiencia eche a perder su día entero.				
18. Usa sus experiencias para ayudarle a decidir cómo actuar.				
19. Evita meterse en problemas.				
20. Resuelve los problemas con sus amistades sin tener que pelear.				

Comentarios: _____

_____

Behavior Management Plan

SAMPLE SELF-CONTROL CURRICULUM BEHAVIOR MANAGEMENT PLAN

STUDENT: Louis Jones   **AGE:** 12   **DATE:** April 16, 2002

TEACHER: Ms. Henderson   **SCHOOL:** George Washington Elementary

Self-Control Goal: To manage stress

Self-Control Skill: To tolerate frustration

Self-Control Objective: When presented with a challenging assignment, Louis will complete the task with minimal teacher assistance.

Student Motivators/Skills/Interests: Verbal praise and peer acceptance; fourth grade reading skills and third grade writing skills; math is his strongest academic area. Louis enjoys reading poems and favors action-adventure stories.

Activities/Lessons/Routines: Louis will be paired with a classmate for creative writing assignments. Action-adventure is a recommended theme. Selections from children's literature that build on his interests, such as Shel Silverstein poems, *Hatchet* by Gary Paulsen, and other adventure stories will augment regular curriculum reading materials. Louis will participate in a mathematics cross-age tutoring program.

Problem Behaviors: Louis often refuses to finish classroom assignments. He argues with other students and teacher.

Positive Behavioral Supports: Sane messages—accept and acknowledge Louis' feelings. Describe the disruptive behavior, tell him why it is disruptive, and describe an alternative behavior. Avoid power struggles by planned ignoring of non-compliance, shortened assignments, and use of logical consequences—for example, work not completed in school must be finished for homework. Enlist parental support. Intermittent verbal praise for completed work.

Comments: Louis needs to experience success in order to persevere in reading and writing. When he completes an assignment, such as presenting a poem to the class, his behavior and peer relationships improve markedly. Louis responds favorably to one-on-one tutoring. Provide ample opportunities for student-centered learning, such as cooperative learning groups and classroom discussions. Give him classroom responsibilities.

SELF-CONTROL CURRICULUM
BEHAVIOR MANAGEMENT PLAN

STUDENT: _____   AGE: _____   DATE: _____

TEACHER : _____   SCHOOL: _____

Self-Control Goal:

Self-Control Skill:

Self-Control Objective:

Student Motivators/Skills/Interests:

Activities/Lessons/Routines:

Problem Behaviors:

Positive Behavioral Supports:

Comments:

Standardization of Self-Control Inventory

Fifteen teachers participated in the standardization of the Self-Control Inventory (SCI). Six of the teachers taught secondary students, the remaining nine taught elementary-age students. All of the teachers had a minimum of 5 years' teaching experience and all teachers except one were participating members in the Preventive Discipline Project from its inception. The 20 self-control skills that make up the Self-Control Curriculum and that are listed in the Self-Control Inventory were validated over a 3-year period. Data was collected through anecdotal observation, behavior checklists, and behavior frequency charts. Analysis was ongoing. Project teachers met two to three times a year to analyze data. Identified skills were contrasted with skills described in *Children Who Hate* (Redl and Wineman, 1951). Group consensus was required for the inclusion of each self-control skill in the curriculum.

The SCI was standardized on 110 students who were identified as having behavior disorders or emotional disturbance by their respective school systems. All of the students had been referred primarily because of aggressive behavior. The student population was culturally diverse with 85 male and 25 female students representing both urban and suburban settings.

Male students ranged in age from 7–18; females ranged in age from 9–21. The average age of males was 12.53 (S.D. = 2.57); average age of females was 13.52 (S.D. = 3.41). Cronbach's Alpha was used to estimate internal reliability of the instrument. Internal consistency coefficient for males and females is 0.62; internal consistency coefficient for males is 0.73. The SCI is gender sensitive, so caution should be used when interpreting results with female students.

The SCI was standardized using a population of students with behavioral and emotional problems. It does not meet psychometric criteria for diagnosis of emotional disturbance, conduct disorder, or any DSM-IV category. The SCI is a valid and reliable *curriculum-based assessment tool* for identifying student strengths and weaknesses in self-control. Reliability is enhanced by independent assessment by two or more professionals who are familiar with the student.

PREVENTIVE DISCIPLINE PROJECT TEACHERS

Ann Boskiewicz, Agawam Junior High School, Agawam, MA

Kate Dean, Sullivan School, Holyoke, MA

Joanne Duval, Juniper Park School, Westfield, MA

Andrea Finnerty, Kelly School, Holyoke, MA

Kathryn Garfield, South Elementary School, Windsor Locks, CT

Maria Halpin, Westfield Middle School, Westfield, MA

Pam Hesseltine, The Key Program, Springfield, MA

Mary Jirkovsky, John J. Lynch Middle School, Holyoke, MA

David Pare, Forest Park Middle School, Springfield, MA

Susan Provoda, Agawam Middle School, Agawam, MA

Linda Redmond, Dorman School, Springfield, MA

AnnMarie Samble, Glickman School, Springfield, MA

Lee Steele, Hillcrest Educational Center, Pittsfield, MA

Susan Therrien, South Elementary School, Windsor Locks, CT

Susan Van Steemburg, Reid Middle School, Pittsfield, MA

Psychometrician—James Martin-Rehrmann, Ph.D., Westfield State College, Westfield, MA

Media Specialist—Mary Giarrusso, Westfield, MA

For more information regarding The Self-Control Curriculum and Self-Control Inventory, write to Martin Henley, Pegasus Center for Education, P.O. Box 1472, Westfield, MA 01086; (413) 572-5320; e-mail PegasusEdu@aol.com

Make the Most of Your Professional Development Investment

Let Solution Tree (formerly National Educational Service) schedule time for you and your staff with leading practitioners in the areas of:

- **Professional Learning Communities** with Richard DuFour, Robert Eaker, Rebecca DuFour, and associates
- **Effective Schools** with associates of Larry Lezotte
- **Assessment for Learning** with Rick Stiggins and associates
- **Crisis Management and Response** with Cheri Lovre
- **Classroom Management** with Lee Canter and associates
- **Discipline With Dignity** with Richard Curwin and Allen Mendler
- **PASSport to Success** (parental involvement) with Vickie Burt
- **Peacemakers** (violence prevention) with Jeremy Shapiro

Additional presentations are available in the following areas:

- At-Risk Youth Issues
- Bullying Prevention/Teasing and Harassment
- Team Building and Collaborative Teams
- Data Collection and Analysis
- Embracing Diversity
- Literacy Development
- Motivating Techniques for Staff and Students

Solution Tree

304 West Kirkwood Avenue
Bloomington, IN 47404-5131
(812) 336-7700
(800) 733-6786 (toll free)
FAX (812) 336-7790
e-mail: info@solution-tree.com
www.solution-tree.com

NEED MORE COPIES OR ADDITIONAL RESOURCES ON THIS TOPIC?

Need more copies of this book? Want your own copy? Need additional resources on this topic? If so, you can order additional materials by using this form or by calling us toll free at (800) 733-6786 or (812) 336-7700. Or you can order by FAX at (812) 336-7790, or visit our Web site at www.solution-tree.com.

Title	Price*	Quantity	Total
Teaching Self-Control	$ 27.95		
Adventure Education for the Classroom Community (curriculum)	89.00		
Anger Management for Youth: Stemming Aggression and Violence	24.95		
The Bullying Prevention Handbook	23.95		
Motivating Students Who Don't Care	9.95		
Reclaiming Our Prodigal Sons and Daughters	18.95		
Reclaiming Youth At Risk	23.95		
Reclaiming Youth At Risk (video set)	295.00		
Teaching Empathy (book and CD)	34.95		
What Do I Do When . . . ? How to Achieve Discipline with Dignity	21.95		
Whatever It Takes: How PLCs Respond When Kids Don't Learn	24.95		
		SUBTOTAL	
		SHIPPING	
Please add 6% of order total. For orders outside the continental U.S., please add 8% of order total.			
		HANDLING	
Please add $4. For orders outside the continental U.S., please add $6.			
		TOTAL (U.S. funds)	

*Price subject to change without notice.

❏ Check enclosed   ❏ Purchase order enclosed
❏ Money order   ❏ VISA, MasterCard, Discover, or American Express (circle one)

Credit Card No._____ Exp. Date _____

Cardholder Signature _____

SHIP TO:

First Name_____ Last Name _____

Position_____

Institution Name _____

Address _____

City_____ State_____ ZIP _____

Phone_____ FAX _____

E-mail _____

Solution Tree (formerly National Educational Service)
304 West Kirkwood Avenue
Bloomington, IN 47404
(812) 336-7700 ● (800) 733-6786 (toll free)
FAX (812) 336-7790
e-mail: orders@solution-tree.com ● www.solution-tree.com